"Kudos to Tracy Duberman and Bob Sachs for [developing such an impactful] and productive approach to help leaders succeed [in] defining moments by enhancing collaboration a[nd...] any executive coach looking to support and inspi[re...] across, this is the essential playbook."

Multimillion-selling author or editor of 39 books, including
Triggers *and* What Got You Here Won't Get You There

"If nothing else, my 25 years in healthcare as a frontline provider, physician leader, health plan executive, and health system executive have convinced me that meaningful transformation of the United States healthcare system is a team sport. The ecosystem is simply too vast and complex to allow for significant success in silos. This timely book is both informative and optimistic. It not only details the leadership traits required to drive meaningful change—more important, it lays out inspiring examples of where this is happening today, what can be learned, and, most critically, what can be cultivated."

David G. Carmouche, MD
President, Ochsner Health Network
Senior Vice President of Community Care, Ochsner Health System

"This book is a must-have for today's leaders to navigate and be successful in healthcare. In our dynamic times of change, the book reviews the whys and hows of collaboration while unmasking and realizing the potential synergies among both related and distinct stakeholders. The Key Takeaways in each chapter provide a roadmap for practical implementation and obtaining desired results. It is a go-to guide for every leader at the forefront of change."

Poonam Alaigh, MD
Executive Vice President of Corporate Development
Remedy Partners

"*From Competition to Collaboration* opens needed dialogue across the spectrum of care delivery. This book is a thought-provoking and practical piece for healthcare executives."

Carman Ciervo, DO
Chief Physician Executive
Jefferson Health New Jersey

"This is a must-read for all of us in the healthcare field who are working to make a difference in the lives and well-being of the communities we serve. It lays out an excellent, practical approach to effectively bring individuals and disparate groups together to resolve key issues that keep us from achieving our Triple Aim goals. It offers the opportunity to personally assess one's readiness to move into the population health world of the future. Worth every penny!"

Michael H. Covert, FACHE
Former CEO, Catholic Health Initiatives, Texas Division
CEO, Covert and Company

"Tracy Duberman and Bob Sachs lay out well-developed methods for health industry leaders to be significantly more effective in today's ever-changing health landscape. As they describe the components of their health ecosystem leadership model, their focus on real-world experiences and thoughtful case studies create a roadmap for anyone who aspires to transform outcomes in health—not just healthcare—by bringing together cross-sector actors to improve the lives of individuals and communities alike."

Matt Guy
Senior Project Consultant
ReThink Health

"I'd like to thank Robert Sachs and Tracy Duberman for capturing, in a concise manner, the nature of what we are doing in the health ecosystem. Driving value is not just a tagline—it's an actionable event. By transforming ourselves, we transform others, taking the well-being of our nation seriously. Well done!"

Donna Mills
Executive Director
Central Oregon Health Council

"The healthcare system is under a period of dynamic change in which issues of affordability, cost, and value are rising to the forefront. It's more important than ever to engage across the ecosystem and work together in pursuit of a common vision and shared, innovative health solutions. *From Competition to Collaboration: How Leaders Cultivate Partnerships to Drive Value and Transform Health* reveals the framework, mind-set, capabilities, and skills needed for leaders to drive change, partner effectively, and improve the health of our communities."

Joshua J. Ofman, MD, MSHS
Senior Vice President, Global Value, Access, and Policy
Amgen

"This essential book highlights the why, what, how, and who for enhancing cross-sector collaboration throughout the health ecosystem—whether at the individual, departmental, organizational, or industry level. Tracy Duberman and Bob Sachs combine years of health industry leadership development experience into a progressive and practical approach that finally enables leaders to drive value and transform health. Their wisdom has shaped and continues to shape my own approach to leading across the health ecosystem leadership model."

Lorie K. Shoemaker, RN, DHA, NEA-BC
Division Senior Vice President and Chief Nursing Officer
Catholic Health Initiatives, St. Luke's Health System

From
Competition
to
Collaboration

ACHE Management Series

From Competition *to* Collaboration

How Leaders Cultivate Partnerships to Drive Value and Transform Health

Tracy L. Duberman
Robert H. Sachs

ACHE Management Series

Your board, staff, or clients may also benefit from this book's insight. For more information on quantity discounts, contact the Health Administration Press Marketing Manager at (312) 424-9450.

23   22   21   20   19   5   4   3   2   1

Library of Congress Cataloging-in-Publication Data
Names: Duberman, Tracy L., author. | Sachs, Robert, 1950- author.
Title: From competition to collaboration : how leaders cultivate
    partnerships to drive value and transform health / Tracy L. Duberman and
    Robert Sachs.
Description: Chicago, IL : Health Administration Press, [2018] | Includes
    bibliographical references.
Identifiers: LCCN 2018028355 (print) | LCCN 2018041362 (ebook) | ISBN
    9781640550216 (ebook) | ISBN 9781640550223 (xml) | ISBN 9781640550230 (
    epub) | ISBN 9781640550247 (mobi) | ISBN 9781640550209 (pbk. : alk. paper)
Subjects: LCSH: Public health administration. | Leadership.
Classification: LCC RA427 (ebook) | LCC RA427 .D79 2018 (print) | DDC
    362.1068--dc23
LC record available at https://lccn.loc.gov/2018028355

Acquisitions editor: Jennette McClain; Project manager: Theresa L. Rothschadl; Cover designer: Brad Norr; Layout: PerfecType

Found an error or a typo? We want to know! Please e-mail it to hapbooks@ache.org, mentioning the book's title and putting "Book Error" in the subject line.

For photocopying and copyright information, please contact Copyright Clearance Center at www.copyright.com or at (978) 750-8400.

Health Administration Press
A division of the Foundation of the American
    College of Healthcare Executives
300 S. Riverside Plaza, Suite 1900
Chicago, IL 60606–6698
(312) 424-2800

Dedication

This book is dedicated to future health ecosystem leaders who will, through collaboration, courage, and commitment, create meaningful solutions to enhance the health of our nation.

Contents

Detailed Contents

Foreword

Amy C. Edmondson
Novartis Professor of Leadership and Management
Harvard Business School

This timely and important book is about innovation that can dramatically improve lives. Not the kind of innovation, unfortunately, in which a new-to-the-world product or service offers previously unimaginable benefits that make prior offerings obsolete. Much as we naturally long for silver bullets and magic wands, "fixing" healthcare will not take the form of a simple solution, no matter how brilliant or innovative. Fixing healthcare means nothing less than reinventing the system—which calls for a new kind of leadership. Appropriately, *From Competition to Collaboration* is a book about what leaders can do to help transform the healthcare ecosystem.

I had the privilege of working with Bob Sachs for nearly a decade in the design and delivery of an annual intensive leadership program for Kaiser Permanente managers at Harvard Business School, and I benefited immensely from his deep industry experience and insight about leadership development. More recently, I worked with Tracy Duberman on two hospital leadership programs and found her enthusiasm and brains to be a powerful combination. It is to the advantage of everyone that these two leadership experts have teamed up to write this book.

Tracy and Bob's book is *timely* because we're running out of time. Healthcare in the United States is broken—and everyone close to the industry knows it. There is no need to repeat the many statistics here (concisely reviewed in the pages that follow), but they neatly add up to spending more and getting less. This book is *important* because it points us in the only direction with the potential to transform the industry: cross-sector collaboration. What must be done is simple. But simple does not mean easy. That is why leadership is so crucial, more crucial than ever. Leadership has always been the force that helps us accomplish challenging goals, and the invitation to exercise that force has never been more real or more compelling than it is today.

Leading across the health ecosystem offers a model of leadership that is desperately needed if we are to create the future of this vital industry in a way that works, promoting health, not just care of the sick. At the very core of Tracy and Bob's model is the need for a new mind-set, which helps drive new collaborative behaviors. This ecosystem mind-set starts with the premise that no sector, on its own, can unravel the Gordian knot of our massive healthcare spending and disappointing outcomes. It is a mind-set that embraces systems thinking, highlighting the fallacy of simple causal relationships and reactive approaches, to help us think differently about the challenges ahead. It recognizes that solutions will come from new collaborative behavior—what I've called *teaming*—among experts from multiple sectors. Because this kind of teaming is hard, as I've documented previously (Edmondson 2012; Edmondson and Salter Reynolds 2016), it rarely happens without a powerful shared purpose and a belief that exciting new possibilities can be created together.

Inside more and more of today's organizations, teaming is recognized as part of the day-to-day work (Edmondson 2012). Teaming is also used to surmount seemingly impossible challenges in crisis situations, where people have teamed up across geographic, social, and cultural boundaries to get the job done (Edmondson 2017). But for teaming in the healthcare ecosystem, the distances between players' mind-sets and skill sets are greater than for cross-functional teamwork in a company, and it also lacks the finite, all-out push that fuels an effective crisis response. The boundaries are more difficult to cross. Goals and incentives are more often at odds. Sustaining energy is even harder. Again, leadership needed!

Making progress in improving both health and care, as Tracy and Bob have argued, necessarily calls for an iterative approach. In other words, there is no blueprint that can be developed in the sterile confines of a conference room and then neatly rolled out by the many organizations and experts who play crucial roles in the industry. There will never be a static master plan for the US health system but rather a constantly shifting set of collaborative activities aimed at producing healthier lives and more affordable care. This iterative, cross-sectoral approach requires that we start to welcome and celebrate experiments, with new initiatives, pilots, partnerships, and other creative ideas to find what works and what does not.

Fortunately, even if the system will never have a single blueprint to guide it forward, leaders do have access to a formula that works. The healthcare ecosystem leadership model is such a formula, and leaders who adopt it with passionate intent will be poised to address both the challenges and the opportunities of teaming across sectors to transform healthcare.

REFERENCES

Edmondson, A. C. 2012. *Teaming: How Organizations Learn, Innovate, and Compete in the Knowledge Economy.* San Francisco: Jossey-Bass.

Edmondson, A. C., and S. Salter Reynolds. 2016. *Building the Future: Big Teaming for Audacious Innovation.* Oakland, CA: Berrett-Koehler Publishers.

Edmondson, A. C., and J. F. Harvey. 2017. *Extreme Teaming: Lessons in Complex, Cross-Sector Leadership.* Bingley, United Kingdom: Emerald Publishing.

Foreword

George Halvorson
Chairman and CEO
Institute for InterGroup Understanding

The United States spends more on healthcare, by a huge percentage, than any other industrialized nation in the world—yet we pale in comparison on most major indicators of good health. In 2009, I wrote a book that described American healthcare as a well-fed non-system of immense size and scope that had the potential to damage our economy badly. I discussed the critical need to use what we know about treatment and prevention to reduce the care burden. Since that time, I am happy to say, there has been some progress. We have seen changes in the way we buy and deliver care, and more people are covered by insurance than ever before.

These changes have started to move us in the right direction. But we are still a very long way from where we need to be. The problems facing the health industry today are far too complex and wide-ranging for any one sector to solve independently. Tracy Duberman and Bob Sachs argue, and I agree, that the solutions needed to change healthcare and health outcomes significantly start with leaders who embody a clear vision and who demonstrate the skills required to work collaboratively across multiple and disparate sectors in the industry. The authors provide a framework for this new type of leadership and a nautical chart to enable these innovators to navigate the choppy waters of ecosystem collaboration. They define the skills and capabilities required for health ecosystem leadership and offer concrete and actionable techniques for development.

Rather than working in their own silos, the sectors must operate interdependently to deliver on critical imperatives such as affordability and access. Though this need is not a simple call to action, organizations across the health ecosystem are stepping up, starting to develop collaborations, and beginning to realize the value of cross-sector partnerships. As this book points out, building and managing these solutions are possible with leaders who see value in working together and have the skills to build the required alignment.

I worked closely with Bob to build the capability of leaders during my 12 years as chairman and CEO of Kaiser Permanente. I have always appreciated his wisdom, his insights, and his ability to get to the heart of what really matters. I am happy to see he has continued to focus his energy on building the capabilities of health leaders through his work with Tracy. Bob and Tracy (who has devoted her career to designing practical and innovative talent development solutions for leaders across the health ecosystem) have used their shared experiences and leadership expertise to collaborate on this timely and important book.

The authors do an excellent job of showing the importance of leading across the health ecosystem, and they illustrate, through real examples and a case study, what ecosystem leadership looks like in action. You will find their guide to developing the leadership skills needed for success practical and immediately useful.

If you are committed to improving our system of care and improving the health of our communities, this book is worth your time and attention. I recommend you read it and use it to develop your health ecosystem leadership skills.

Acknowledgments

Much like the health ecosystem solutions we write about, this book is truly a collaborative labor of love. We are deeply grateful to several individuals for helping us take an idea we surfaced at a The Leadership Development (TLD) Group board meeting and cultivating it into the reality of this book. These individuals gave of themselves generously during our brainstorming phase, our research phase, and the writing and editing phases. While there are far too many to mention by name (you know who you are), we would like to acknowledge the following people formally.

Our TLD Group team:

- *Kim Rubenstein.* Your research prowess, project planning, and execution skills are the best, bar none. You are a force to be reckoned with. Watch out, world.
- *Amy Riemer.* You introduced the original "crazy" idea, simply stated as, "Hey, let's write a book!" We're quite sure that without your persistence, this idea would have stayed just that—a great idea.
- *Tara Satlow and Lisa Clarke.* You are the quintessential thought partners and powerhouse editors.
- *Our TLD Group advisory board (past and present).* Your commitment to us, your support for the work we do, and the passion with which you serve our industry are incomparable.

Our Sherpa, Graham Schofield, bravely accepted the challenge to work with not one, but two first-time book authors. Thank you. You read our white papers, watched our videos, listened to us on tape, and spent hours with us on video conference to cocreate a coherent narrative.

Our spouses, children, extended families, and friends lost us for a while as we dedicated our "free time" to research, writing, and editing. For this, we are eternally grateful.

We would like to thank our clients for sharing your challenges and allowing us to support you on your leadership journey. You inspire us each and every day.

Finally, we must make special mention of the following pioneers of health ecosystem leadership who agreed to be interviewed and allowed us to share their wisdom here. In alphabetical order, they are the following:

- Poonam Alaigh, MD, MSHCPM, FACP, former Acting Undersecretary for Health at the US Department of Veterans Affairs and current Executive Vice President of Corporate Development at Remedy Partners, Inc.
- Andrew Baskin, Vice President, National Medical Director for Quality and Clinical Policy at Aetna
- Tanisha Carino, PhD, former Vice President of US Public Policy at GSK and current Executive Director at FasterCures (a center of the Milken Institute)
- David Carmouche, MD, Senior Vice President of Ochsner Health System and President of Ochsner Health Network in Louisiana
- Carman Ciervo, DO, FACOFP, Executive Vice President and Chief Physician Executive at Jefferson Health New Jersey
- Mohamed Diab, MD, former Vice President of Provider Transformation at Aetna and current President and CEO at ActiveHealth Management

- Robert C. Garrett, Co-CEO of Hackensack Meridian Health
- Matt Guy, President and Owner of Accelerated Transformation Associates
- Bob Hemker, retired former President and CEO of Palomar Health
- Andrew Horowitz, Founder and CEO, Enclara Pharmacia
- John K. Lloyd, Co-CEO of Hackensack Meridian Health
- Roland Lyon, President of Kaiser Foundation Health Plan of Colorado
- Julie Miller-Phipps, President of Kaiser Foundation Hospitals and Health Plan in Southern California
- Donna Mills, Executive Director of Central Oregon Health Council
- Joshua J. Ofman, MD, MSHS, Senior Vice President of Global Value, Access, and Policy at Amgen
- Barry H. Ostrowsky, President and CEO of RWJBarnabas Health
- Craig Samitt, MD, MBA, Executive Vice President, and CEO of Blue Cross and Blue Shield of Minnesota
- Lorie K. Shoemaker, RN, DHA, NEA-BC, Senior Vice President and Chief Nursing Officer at Catholic Health Initiatives, Texas Division
- Joe Wilkins, MBA, FACHE, Senior Vice President and Chief Transformation Officer at Atlantic Health System
- Patrick R. Young, President of Population Health for Hackensack Meridian Health

Introduction

*There is nothing more difficult to take in hand, more perilous
to conduct, or more uncertain in its success, than to take
the lead in the introduction of a new order of things.*

—Niccolo Machiavelli, 1513

No one can deny that the US health industry is in a state of
upheaval. Rising costs of care, limited access, variable coverage,
and less-than-optimal health outcomes have become catchphrases
typifying the industry. While efforts are being made to address
these challenges and respond to shifting government regulations,
they have resulted in mostly patchwork solutions that are reactive
and focused on the short term. As such, the impact is often less
than ideal and often ineffective. Meanwhile, demand for services
continues to grow as the population ages and chronic (and costly)
diseases continue to exert pressure on the industry.

These challenges are just some of what we'll address in this book.
One of our key messages is that to make any truly meaningful
change, we need to think very differently about how we approach
the business of healthcare—we must adopt a broader purpose. By
that we mean a different—and much bigger—focus on promoting
wellness. We are suggesting a shift from health*care* to *health* and

care. And because care, while important, is a relatively small factor in population health, we believe working across the overall health ecosystem—a body of interconnected stakeholders—will advance the shared mission of improving the health of populations.

As we try to find methods to better align and focus on health across the sectors of the industry, the leadership demands will continue to rise and become ever more challenging. That's the environment we're in, and the benefits that can be attained by working together and across boundaries are vital to the solution.

Marc Scheinrock and colleagues (2016) refer to "predictive maintenance and keeping people well." They suggest that while an emphasis on wellness helps to keep people focused on their personal health, it also has the potential to improve bottom lines. In helping to drive up the quality of life, organizations can leverage cost reductions, with the results being healthier individuals *and* an improved return on investment (ROI). Improved population health can be viewed as an ongoing shared-value proposition—a cause and effect that can engender continuous improvements in ROI (exhibit I.1).

Exhibit I.1: Shared-Value Proposition and ROI

Costs

Quality of life

The role that leaders play in aligning organizations toward the common goal of keeping the population healthy is at the center of this book. Strong partnerships across multiple industry sectors are critical in dealing with the various forces that have the potential to push things in the wrong direction, and we are actively seeking to encourage connections and dialogue across sectors and among stakeholders. We will espouse an ecosystem view and demonstrate that, done well, this perspective can help make some very significant differences in overall population health—in the right direction.

We believe an ecosystem perspective is vital given the myriad issues the industry currently faces. It sets the stage for dealing with tensions and conflicts that occur between sectors, whether they're providers and payers, physicians and hospitals, pharmaceuticals and clinicians, or other permutations. There are significant differences in the structure, organizational strategy, and work processes across the various health sectors that need to be addressed, and the ecosystem approach provides a framework for how we can lead the industry to be both efficient and effective.

We are confident that an ecosystem approach will create innovation and scalable solutions that are simply not possible when working only in sector silos. To go beyond those boundaries, the challenge is how to capitalize on shared interests while, at the same time, tending to the interests of each organization or sector. This equilibrium requires each set of players to think about what's most critical to them, what's less important, and what can be done differently to achieve a common purpose.

With such balancing and leveraging, there's an opportunity to begin to create new and different operating systems collectively. As we have already stated, establishing these to achieve the shared goals of the health ecosystem requires diverse organizations to reach agreements that support their efforts to work together. As stated by Mark R. Kramer and Mark W. Pfitzer (2016), while it is critical, this proposition is not simple:

Even corporations once known for a hard-nosed approach have embarked on significant shared value initiatives. But as they pursue shared value strategies, businesses inevitably face barriers at many turns.

No company operates in isolation; each exists in an ecosystem where societal conditions may curtail its markets and restrict the productivity of its suppliers and distributors. Government policies present their own limitations, and cultural norms also influence demand.

These conditions are beyond the control of any company—or of any single actor. To advance shared value efforts, therefore, businesses must foster and participate in multisector coalitions—and for that, they need a new framework.

Such a framework is at the heart of this book; in developing our thinking, we have been struck by how the complexity of being able to work and lead multisector partnerships rises significantly. How do you take the competencies and capabilities that have enabled leaders to be successful in their own organizations and spread them across a much more complex environment, where shared history, values, or mission don't yet exist?

As Kramer and Pfitzer (2016) suggest, the common denominator is the creation of shared value. The pathway is the mind-set and skill set that leaders need to develop and use to establish the conditions for *real* success. It's all about seemingly disparate organizations working together in different ways, engaging with each other in pursuit of a common vision. Because the diversity and competing interests of the involved players increases, pursuit of the vision gets harder and creates a pressing need for new and distinctly different leadership skills.

In this book, we offer an introduction to and explanation of our framework—our *health ecosystem leadership model* (HELM)©. This model has been developed over the past few years and is based on what we have learned from our work with health industry leaders who have been the pioneers of an ecosystem approach. It is their hard-won successes that have driven our learning.

These leaders foster what we refer to as an *ecosystem mind-set*—an understanding of the importance of bringing together traditionally disparate organizations from the different health sectors to create shared, innovative health solutions. Throughout the book, you will see quotes from personal interviews we conducted with leaders who provide great examples of ecosystem leadership in action. They collectively demonstrate how they have sought to implement the solutions we advocate and help corroborate our model.

This ecosystem mind-set is well illustrated by Craig Samitt, MD, MBA, current CEO of Blue Cross and Blue Shield of Minnesota and former executive vice president and chief clinical officer at Anthem, Inc., a health insurance company headquartered in Indiana. Craig notes:

> All players in the ecosystem share the goal of providing higher quality, more accessible, more affordable care to the people we serve. Everyone talks about that as an aspiration, but there are very few organizations that have executed upon it because execution of the Triple Aim to some extent requires reinvention of each of the players.
>
> It feels that all the distinct players in the ecosystem have done what they can do within their world to drive industry change. Unless we begin to see partnerships with shared accountability and coordination of functions across the various players, we're not going to advance to the next level. It's time for a new model.

Our overall perspective is drawn from many decades of experience working as executives in various sectors of the health industry, in addition to our depth of expertise designing talent strategies to execute business strategy. Having developed the model, we felt compelled to share it. That is our reason for writing this book—if you're reading it, then you too believe in the need for the ecosystem approach.

We present our HELM model and practical suggestions for how to develop health ecosystem leadership to allow you and your fellow executives to collaborate across sectors effectively. We've defined the required skill sets and put forth recommendations for how to develop and use these skills. Among other things, you will learn how to

- recognize the essential building blocks of cross-sector leadership,
- develop your leadership behaviors to create the pathways for building cross-sector partnerships,
- collaborate effectively with others and demonstrate the HELM behaviors in pursuit of common goals, and
- establish measures for success to guide and assess the benefit of action.

Having set the stage, we hope you find immense value in the pages to follow. After reading this book, we hope you will share our ideas and recommendations with leaders in your organization, your sector, and your broader health ecosystem. Our industry needs a good deal of help and support if it is to make the progress needed toward the changes that are essential, and we believe that, through this book, we offer much toward these vital goals.

To your success and the health and wellness of our country,

Tracy Duberman
President, The Leadership Development Group

Bob Sachs
Board Chair, The Leadership Development Group

REFERENCES

Kramer, M. R., and M. W. Pfitzer. 2016. "The Ecosystem of Shared Value." *Harvard Business Review*. Published October 1. https:// hbr.org/2016/10/the-ecosystem-of-shared-value.

Scheinrock, M., R. Bush, J. Lee, and H. Greenspun. 2016. "Bending the Cost Curve for Healthcare Providers: When Traditional Approaches Aren't Enough." Deloitte. Published June 14. www2 .deloitte.com/us/en/pages/dbriefs-webcasts/events/june /2016/dbriefs-bending-the-cost-curve-for-health-care-providers -when-traditional-approaches-arent-enough.html.

CHAPTER 1

A New Focus—A Different Way Forward

Growth is the only evidence of life.

—John Henry Newman, 1864

A SYSTEM DESIGNED FOR A DIFFERENT TIME

While the health of the US population trails that of most other developed countries, which pay less per capita than we do, healthcare costs are at an all-time high, either directly competing with basic needs such as housing and food or becoming a barrier to any access at all. Every US healthcare executive knows that the industry is in desperate need of repair, yet the path to *real* change is relatively unexplored. The industry's focus on value is a noble one, and the path to controlling costs while enhancing quality requires significant transformation in all sectors that affect health and wellness— certainly a most audacious goal.

Increasingly, we recognize that to take on these challenges and make a lasting impact, we need to expand our focus from health*care* to *health* and *care*, from treating the sick to fostering population health and wellness. In simple terms, this shift means programs and services must focus not only on health per se but on a much broader quality of life.

In defining the concept, public health scholars Jonathan E. Fielding and Steven Teutsch (2017) expand our thinking on the goals of the health system with reference to a World Health Organization report emphasizing that social determinants correlate with health outcomes in the United States. The WHO suggests that the states with the poorest health outcomes cannot improve without addressing problems of poverty, job creation, education, transportation, and the built environment.

Our conversations with senior executives from multiple sectors of the health industry concur with this and indicate that to really affect population health—a hugely complex issue—no single sector can do it alone. Providers and payers need to find ways to work collaboratively, with the goal of creating solutions that work for both sectors *and* the consumers they serve. Life sciences companies need to look at reimbursement schemes with payers and think about how there could be a better match between what drugs are being developed and how they're being reimbursed.

These sectors need to work more with other ecosystem partners such as public health agencies, schools, local and state governments, community services, and other public entities. Initiatives aimed at improving overall population health and well-being need to involve those who can influence the socioeconomic status, education, physical environment, employment, and social support networks that influence health, as well.

As the Centers for Disease Control's Health Disparities Report (2013) stated, poor health status, disease risk factors, and limited access to healthcare are often interrelated and have been reported among persons with social, economic, and environmental disadvantages. The conditions and social context in which persons live can explain, in part, why certain populations in the United States are healthier than others and why some are not as healthy as they could be.

We know that poverty limits access to healthy foods and safe neighborhoods and that better education is a predictor of improved health. We also know that the differences in health are striking in communities with inadequate resources, such as unstable housing, low income, unsafe neighborhoods, or substandard education. By applying what we know about the impact of social determinants (more on this in chapter 3), we can improve individual and population health and also advance health equity.

As costs rise, so does the complexity of leading in a health services organization. Organizations are simultaneously challenged to develop strategies to improve the customer experience, reduce the total cost of care, optimize value-based payment models, enhance coverage and access, and improve population health for all groups. Having all these complexities to deal with reflects why the old system, based on outdated theories, can no longer work. What is required are solutions that span the many sectors of the health ecosystem—a perspective confirmed by Jane Erickson and colleagues (2017, 5), who suggest that "More and more Americans are recognizing that our health and well-being rely on a system designed for a different time, and it is failing us. In response, leaders are organizing in new ways to contend with the many systemic challenges we face, often choosing to form multi-sector partnerships. As longstanding partnerships evolve, and as new ones form across the country, each group must negotiate for themselves a clear reason for being together, as well as practical ways to do business differently."

THE ECOSYSTEM NEEDS DIFFERENT LEADERSHIP

Effective collaboration across sectors will be the key to success, bringing together groups that are diverse in purpose, values, perspectives, culture, expertise, and incentives. Creating solutions with such differing stakeholders requires a leadership focus and skills that reach far beyond what leaders are typically responsible for in their own roles in their own organizations and even in their own sectors. Yet this cross-sector leadership is exactly what's required—it necessitates an entirely new approach to leading that entails new ways of thinking, new ways of partnering, and a new ability to manage competing priorities and the ambiguities that often arise from diverse perspectives.

The changes the industry needs can only occur at an ecosystem level. By the term *ecosystem*, we mean a system of diverse yet interdependent sectors with a shared interest in improving health outcomes and the quality of life. We believe that if you are a health industry leader you need to lead—and lead effectively—*beyond* your organizational boundaries.

While leading across departments within your organization is still essential, to make a real impact on health and cost trends, leaders need to be equipped to drive change in and across sectors. Because this solution space is so much bigger, so are the leadership challenges (see exhibit 1.1).

Talk to any leader in any sector in the healthcare industry and you'll find they all agree that making things better for their consumers is their central focus. Take, for example, these extracts from the

Exhibit 1.1: Ecosystem Leadership Challenges

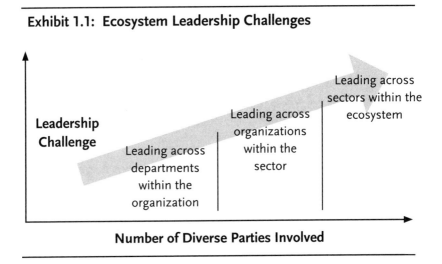

mission statements for a pharmaceutical company, a provider, and a payer organization.

- Our mission is to help people do more, feel better, live longer.
- Designing and delivering high-quality, innovative, personalized healthcare to build healthier communities and improve lives for patients, consumers, and caregivers.
- Together, we are transforming healthcare with trusted and caring solutions.

Can you tell which one belongs to which sector? The answer is that it doesn't matter because the common theme is evident. While all sectors strive to enhance health, each sector addresses that common purpose from its own unique perspective and its own, often competing, priorities. In case you were wondering, the three mission extracts come respectively from GlaxoSmithKline Pharmaceuticals, Atlantic Health System, and Anthem.

Efforts to build innovative collaborative solutions require getting all the different parties together and aligning the stakeholders and their unique perspectives around a common goal. With everyone at the same table, we need find ways for leaders from various sectors to address these collective challenges while still serving their own specific stakeholders.

This view is endorsed by entrepreneur John Geraci (2016): "To adopt what I call an ecosystem mind-set [means to have] an understanding that the keys to new value and growth likely do not reside within one's current boundaries but beyond them, and that success involves forging new connections to solve problems and create new value as a team. It's a mind-set that very few big companies and individuals have, but need." This view, combined with our collective experience, is exactly what led to our research, conducted through our interviews with the leading industry executives previously mentioned.

CASE STUDY

Analysis of our findings has resulted in a cross-sector leadership model designed to develop leaders who can execute business strategies that extend beyond their organization or sector into the broader health industry, working together in ways that affect the shared goal of much-improved population health. Here is one case study, offering an example of how one organization navigated across different sectors.

The Situation

With the implementation of the Affordable Care Act, a leading payer organization realized it would not be able to cover healthcare costs alone and would need to think more broadly. The population it served was overwhelmingly unhealthy, rural, poor, and cared for by primary care providers who were largely unorganized, independent, small, and lacking in electronic records or infrastructure.

The organization's new goal became finding a way to change its relationship with providers to support their ability to care for populations more fully and to be rewarded for good primary care.

The Solution

Working with the provider sector, it designed a program aimed to invest health plan resources into strengthening the relationship between the payer organization and the providers, as well as supporting primary care doctors while allowing them to remain independent. The program involved the creation of an information technology (IT) infrastructure, which included electronic health records (EHRs) and access to clinical and pharmacy claims data, and which pulled in clinical data from EHRs to populate registries.

The Outcome

By the end of the first year, the program had improved the quality of care for all chronic diseases. The registries provided doctors with new insight into enhancing health outcomes and allowed the payer organization to provide care coordination and outreach for the providers.

In addition, the data enabled the payer organization to understand quality and performance metrics and set up a rewards system for physicians who provided outstanding care to patients with chronic diseases. While enhancing health outcomes for members, the organization also reduced the total cost of care per member per month by 20 percent.

VIEWS ON THE HEALTH ECOSYSTEM

While the specific definition of a health ecosystem may vary from organization to organization, the leaders that we quote in this book all refer to two common elements: cross-sector partnerships and collaborative solutions. As an example, David Carmouche, MD, senior vice president of Ochsner Health System and president of Ochsner Health Network, a healthcare provider organization in Louisiana, shared with us how he defines his organization's ecosystem:

> Our ecosystem consists of several sectors that come together to create the environment in which our organization operates:
>
> - The provider sector is made up of the Ochsner Health Network (OHN).
> - For the payer sector, Ochsner Health System is a high-performing network that is viewed as a valuable opportunity for purchasers.

- Whether it's manufacturers; device companies; or pharmaceuticals, these form the health sciences sector.
- The technology and health IT sector has become an increasingly big part of our organizations' ecosystem, whether it's in big data, analytics, consumer engagement, or connectivity.

What David's definition suggests is that, while his organization is in the provider sector of the health industry, it is important to consider the role of other key players and how they contribute to one's own ecosystem.

THE LEADERSHIP CHALLENGE

As we'll discuss in subsequent chapters, taking such a broad and distinctly new approach to leading is not easy. In most organizations, the leaders at the top can resolve conflicts and make the tough decisions. When leaders work across organizations, decision-making is more dispersed, the lines are blurred, and the approach needs to become more collaborative.

A population health approach calls for shared responsibility for health outcomes with multiple sectors whose activities directly or indirectly affect health. To be successful, participants need a clearly stated purpose based on shared values and interests. However, often sectors place value on different things. The aim of collaborative work is to get beyond the differences and find the common ground needed to generate collective action to improve health.

Establishing this shared purpose allows partners to see how participation will help them to achieve their own mandate and contribute to the larger good. Intersectoral action should be viewed as a win–win situation—whereby each party gains something—as opposed to a competitive exercise based on so-called sectoral imperialism, in which a single sector is seen as benefiting from the work of others as it fulfills its own purpose or mandate.

As we'll explore further in chapter 3, collaboration is not easy, as described by authors Amy C. Edmondson and Susan Salter Reynolds (2016, 6): "Future building is hard. . . . This is because bringing together diverse elements to create a functioning whole presents countless ways for integration to break down." As explained in our introduction, our aim is to support theory with practical examples of how effective ecosystem leaders demonstrate a new and different mind-set, as well as new and different leadership behaviors advocated for in our model.

The shift in focus from health*care* to *health* requires an ecosystem perspective, with leaders who see themselves as influencers in the communities in which they serve—where their role is, at a minimum, to bring other sectors together to affect overall health and wellness. This book is focused on this philosophy and how success can be navigated with a change in mind-set and leadership. For example, consider the experience of Julie Miller-Phipps, president of Kaiser Foundation Hospitals and Health Plan in Southern California. She clearly demonstrates the approach of a leader who understands the importance of partnerships as a means toward better population health: "Some of our current top areas of focus are nontraditional aspects of healthcare, such as educational attainment, food stability, job creation, or mental health. We are now broadening our thinking around how to cultivate relationships in the community and pay more attention to the social determinants of care. The ecosystem includes the integration we have within our organization and the communities that we serve."

In the pages to come, we address the challenges and offer solutions with help from leaders who are doing this work with great success. Our interviewees from across the health ecosystem have successfully demonstrated cross-sector collaborative leadership, and we're thrilled to share their successes with you in the rest of the book.

KEY TAKEAWAYS

- The path to controlling costs while enhancing quality requires significant transformation in all sectors that affect health and wellness.
- Improving overall population health and well-being needs to span the many sectors of the health ecosystem and involve those who can influence the socioeconomic status, education, physical environment, employment, and social support networks that affect health.
- Health industry leaders need to demonstrate collaborative, cross-sector leadership to work toward the shared goal of improved population health.
- The shift in focus from health*care* to *health* requires an ecosystem perspective, with leaders who see themselves as influencers in the communities in which they serve, where their role is, at a minimum, to bring other sectors together to foster overall health and wellness.

REFERENCES

Centers for Disease Control and Prevention. 2013. "CDC Health Disparities and Inequalities Report—United States, 2013." *Morbidity and Mortality Weekly Report* 62 (3). www.cdc.gov /mmwr/pdf/other/su6203.pdf.

Edmondson, A. C., and S. Salter Reynolds. 2016. *Building the Future: Big Teaming for Audacious Innovation.* Oakland, CA: Berrett-Koehler Publishers.

Erickson, J., B. Milstein, L. Schafer, K. E. Pritchard, C. Levitz, C. Miller, and A. Cheadle. 2017. *Progress Along the Pathway for Transforming Regional Health: A Pulse Check on Multi-Sector Partnerships.* ReThink Health Press. Published March. www

.rethinkhealth.org/wp-content/uploads/2017/03/2016-Pulse
-Check-Narrative-Final.pdf.

Fielding, J. E., and S. Teutsch. 2017. "Social Determinants of Health: Building Wide Coalitions Around Well-Honed Messages." *American Journal of Public Health* 107 (6): 870–71.

Geraci, J. 2016. "How an Ecosystem Mindset Can Help People and Organizations Succeed." *Harvard Business Review.* Published May 12. www.hbr.org/2016/05/how-an-ecosystem-mindset -can-help-people-and-organizations-succeed.

CHAPTER 2

A Perfect Storm for Change

Change is inevitable. Progress is optional.

—Tony Robbins, 2012

THE NUMBERS ARE TOO BIG

The Centers for Medicare & Medicaid Services (2018) revealed that healthcare expenditures exceeded $3 trillion and account for close to 18 percent of the nation's gross domestic product. Per capita spending was almost $10,000, or 28 times what it had been in 1970. Despite these expenditures, health outcomes in the United States continue to lag behind other developed countries on several key health outcome measures, such as life expectancy, the prevalence of chronic conditions, and mortality from heart disease—the leading cause of death in the United States.

Beyond the current system being too expensive and not producing expected outcomes, we are also grappling with an insurmountable increase in the demand for care as the population grows—people live longer as the rate of chronic diseases increases. Furthermore, we are fully aware that health status is strongly affected by controllable factors, including where we live, our physical environment, our income, our education level, and our relationships with friends and family.

THE SOCIAL DETERMINANTS OF HEALTH

A Robert Wood Johnson Foundation study found that only 20 percent of the factors that influence a person's health are related to access and quality of healthcare, whereas "the other 80 percent are due to socioeconomic, environmental, or behavioral factors—including insufficient housing, poor diet, inadequate exercise, and drug and alcohol use" (Hussein and Collins 2016). In exhibit 2.1, Harry Heiman and Samantha Artiga (2015) from the Kaiser Family Foundation offer a comprehensive view of these key considerations.

Overriding concerns about cost and quality—coupled with a focus on the social determinants of health and wellness—are leading

Exhibit 2.1: Social Determinants of Health

Economic Stability	Neighborhood and Physical Environment	Education	Food	Community and Social Context	Health Care System
Employment	Housing	Literacy	Hunger	Social integration	Health coverage
Income	Transportation	Language	Access to healthy options	Support systems	Provider availability
Expenses	Safety	Early childhood education		Community engagement	Provider linguistic and cultural competency
Debt	Parks	Vocational training		Discrimination	Quality of care
Medical bills	Playgrounds	Higher education			
Support	Walkability				

Health Outcomes
Mortality, Morbidity, Life Expectancy, Health Care Expenditures, Health Status, Functional Limitations

Source: Heiman and Artiga (2015).

us to reorient our thinking from health*care* to *health*. In our work with ecosystem leaders, we are seeing examples of new and innovative approaches to health and wellness. Insurance companies are offering discounts on healthy food choices to their subscribers, pharmaceutical companies are providing access to support groups for customers with specific diseases, and caregivers are sponsoring employment initiatives in the communities they serve.

Here's an example of such an initiative from Barry Ostrowsky, president and CEO of RWJBarnabas Health, a not-for-profit integrated healthcare delivery system in New Jersey:

> In vulnerable communities, employment is the number one social determinant of health. If you don't have a job, you don't have money, and you can't afford all the things you need, including healthy foods and wellness support. As a result, you're unfortunately more likely to develop poor health habits.
>
> We began a program called "Hire Newark," which is essentially an employment boot camp. Each class has 12 people, and these folks agreed to effectively be schooled in everything from how to dress, how to succeed in an interview, how to write and speak in the business environment, etc.
>
> The unique aspect of this program is that it guarantees a job after finishing the 8- to 10-week program. We just graduated our third class, and of the 36 graduates, four of them have already been promoted from their entry-level positions.
>
> It's not just our organization, since a number of other anchor organizations in Newark agreed to employ these graduates as well. What this proves to us is that, even though it's a small project, it can be done. We can make a difference in the lives of people who would otherwise have been chronically unemployed and, as a result, be more likely to have health-related problems.

We, and the pioneers we work with, know that meaningful reductions in healthcare expenditure are a matter of keeping people healthy and out of the delivery system, and in order to do so, we need to take into account the various factors that affect health and promote wellness. However, most healthcare organizations today continue to pay scant attention to these matters. While some may be unaware of the largest controllable issues affecting the health of their communities, more likely most are not incentivized to think outside their four walls to consider the social determinants. Author Ian Morrison (2017) describes the pioneering work of ProMedica, led by CEO Randy Oostra, to address a common social determinant of poor health.

> Research has shown that food insecurity leads to health problems throughout a person's life. Pregnant women who live in food-insecure households are more likely to deliver underweight babies, while children suffer from more ear infections, colds, stomachaches, and iron deficiency. Without an adequate food supply, children also develop more cognitive and physical development problems. In adults, dietary shortfalls and irregular eating patterns can lead to obesity, chronic disease, and behavioral health problems. And seniors who are food insecure experience more disability, less resistance to infection, and longer hospital stays.
>
> These facts led ProMedica to become a pioneer in the use of a food pharmacy (prescribing food as medicine) and investing in inner-city grocery stores with healthy food. ProMedica employees started with a visit to Boston Medical Center's Grow Clinic, a successful program that had been operating for a decade, to learn how to start their own program. They opened the first ProMedica Food Pharmacy in April 2015 in Toledo.
>
> As the ProMedica food security program description states, "The idea of the Food Pharmacy is simple: Food

is medicine. As such, a healthcare professional writes a referral to the food pharmacy for patients that are identified as food insecure. These patients are then able to visit the pharmacy to pick up a supplemental supply of healthy food for their family.

While numerous organizations have stepped up to spearhead exceptional population health initiatives, some organizations may not have the resources or capabilities to drive the solutions. Instead, ecosystem leaders could assume the role of convener or facilitator of these approaches by bringing together stakeholders who can make an impact on a critical need affecting the communities they serve. For example, Bob Hemker, retired president and CEO of Palomar Health, a California healthcare district in San Diego County, demonstrates an understanding of how social determinants affect his organization:

> The bottom line is that we are a provider organization and trying to address issues of population health can be very consuming and detracting from our everyday responsibilities. But we have a comprehensive continuum of care that we can draw from to break away from the traditional boundaries of health*care* to address the social determinants of *health*. We feel that we may not necessarily have to always be the "doer" of a health solution, but perhaps we could assume the role of facilitator to have an impact on population health.
>
> As an example, take the dependency issue between behavioral health and homelessness. We are a primary provider of behavioral health, but we do not have an obligation to build a homeless center. However, homelessness is an important issue to us because it impacts our ED [emergency department] saturation and recidivism rate, but it's not necessarily our problem to solve. Instead, we

ought to collaborate with the public and/or private sectors
to figure out solutions to homelessness.

As the industry shifts to payment models that incent for value, leaders will need to begin to shift to programs and services that reduce
costs while enhancing quality outcomes. This change will drive a
natural focus on the social determinants of health and wellness, but
there will be much more to consider.

Who could argue that the industry isn't facing volatility, uncertainty, complexity, and ambiguity? The bottom line is that there
is presently a perfect storm in the health industry, and it's even
bigger than the issues already discussed. In the following sections,
we'll highlight four critical issues that we consider to be industrial
tsunamis: payment reform, big data, technology, and the rise of
consumerism.

FOUR TSUNAMIS

Payment Reform

The Affordable Care Act (ACA), passed into law in 2010, was
intended to reform the healthcare system by giving more Americans access to quality, affordable health insurance and curbing the
growth of healthcare spending in the United States. To change how
healthcare is organized, delivered, and paid for, the ACA contains
numerous provisions that target the well-known shortcomings of
the US health system, ranging from the inefficiency and high cost of
our predominantly fee-for-service system to the extreme variability
in the quality of care patients receive from region to region.

The shift toward payment based on the value of care provided
is intended to drive new behaviors in an attempt to reduce costs,
enhance quality, and improve the patient experience. While no one
can predict what the next iteration will be, it seems clear that any
new payment models will influence the way healthcare businesses

operate, which affects the ways in which organizations deliver care, providers treat their patients, providers and payers interact, and pharmaceutical companies manufacture drugs.

Over the last five years, the payer teams at Amgen, a biopharmaceutical company headquartered in California, have led the company into the realm of value-based partnerships and innovative payment models. As part of a broader corporate transformation, they have instituted a call to action to create some urgency in the company around becoming a more collaborative partner for other sectors in the health industry.

Josh Ofman, the senior vice president of global value, access, and policy at Amgen, has presented at leadership meetings across the company to try to stimulate recognition of the importance of becoming a more integrated partner and collaborator in our complex healthcare ecosystem. In our interview with Josh, he relates his usual pitch at these events to gain buy-in:

> The healthcare system is under a period of dynamic change where issues of affordability, cost, and value are rising to the forefront. The system is burdened by a tremendous financial strain. The main culprits are the rising cost of disease and the aging population.
>
> The solution to that problem, in many respects, is innovative biopharmaceuticals. But too often we're seen as the problem, and so we have to change the conversation within the ecosystem to recognize that innovative biopharmaceuticals are part of that solution, and in order to get that done we have to become an integrated, collaborative partner in this health ecosystem so that we're not seen simply as a supplier.

The challenges arising from the significant changes in business operations naturally result in a call for a different type of leadership—one that thinks of work as a collaboration. Senior executives will have to develop expertise in areas of healthcare that they may previously have considered beyond their bailiwick and work comfortably with others on new terrain. This point is explored by HCL Technologies (2011, 4–5):

> The new paradigm reflects a "systems thinking" view of an industry where the walls separating stakeholders are steadily crumbling—where the success of one depends on the success of others, and where new business models of coexistence and codevelopment are rapidly becoming the norm.
>
> That's partly due to new government regulations that have opened up vast flows of information between patients, providers, and payers—and throughout the ecosystem— and partly the result of runaway medical costs, which have spurred the entire complex to live within its means. That priority demands more collaboration, more information sharing, more interoperability, and more integration. In short: more convergence.

Big Data

Our industry is inundated with data that only become meaningful information when processed, organized, and interpreted. Expectations for the speed at which data become meaningful are increasing at an exponential rate with the huge growth in data availability—the conundrum of big data. The explosion of big data constitutes a second tsunami in the health industry, where executives, providers, clinical researchers, and others are facing never-before-seen torrents of new numbers and are on a sharp learning curve to shape it into something meaningful. Leaders looking to create value and quality through predictive analytics face significant challenges.

All sectors of the health industry have access to data on outcomes, quality, safety, patient satisfaction, and employee engagement. Increasingly, consumers have access to these data points as well, allowing them to make cost and quality decisions. Data availability also creates opportunities for organizations to effectively align, interpret, and act on information to drive performance, enhancing efforts to improve health, cost, and quality—think the Triple Aim. Take, for example, the transformational work led by Patrick Young, president of population health at Hackensack Meridian Health, a leading not-for-profit, integrated delivery system in New Jersey:

> When I came to this organization there was a lot of data. The question was: How did we make that useful and how did we get it to physicians in a timely and appropriate manner? We decided to develop our own data warehouse so we could control the clinical data, to gather and store what we collect in real time through our electronic medical records.
>
> Covering items such as claims data from payers, pharmacy data, background information, etc., all of these different pieces of information came together in one location to give us a complete view of our patients. We're now utilizing that information to work with our care managers and have also begun some predictive modeling.
>
> Based on the information we have, we are able to identify potential issues for patients. Our data analytics team—clinical pharmacists, population health scientists, data analysts, etc.—provide our physicians and care managers with this information so they can reach out to patients proactively. This has led to some great outcomes.
>
> For example, we had a congestive heart failure patient who tracked and sent her daily vital signs through an iPad provided by our care managers. Her assigned care manager was able to track this patient's progress and proactively intervene if any readings were cause for concern. This novel approach reduced this patient's hospital admissions and enabled her to lead a more active life. The current challenge is effectively organizing and facilitating meaningful use for the data we have.

Clearly, it takes effort to maximize the return on all the available data. That brings us to the next big issue.

Technology

Technology is transforming the industry at lightning speed. Breakthroughs in research, treatments, and communications have given industry executives, researchers, medical providers, and consumers new tools to work with and fresh ways to deliver and receive care.

In addition, all sectors in the industry—providers, payers, and pharmaceutical companies—are using social media to establish contact with current and future consumers, launch public awareness campaigns, and perform community outreach. Some sophisticated sites even offer instant chats with nurses and doctors about medical issues and reminders to obtain regularly needed tests, medications, and vaccinations.

Technology has changed healthcare by providing new diagnostic and caregiving tools, medicines, and treatments that save lives and improve recovery for billions. For example, in our interview with Robert Garrett, co-CEO of Hackensack Meridian Health, he discussed the innovative partnership between his organization and the New Jersey Innovation Institute, a wholly owned not-for-profit subsidiary of the New Jersey Institute of Technology: "In partnership with the New Jersey Innovation Institute, an affiliate of the state's largest technology university, we launched the state's first incubator to improve healthcare [Agile Strategies Lab]. The network contributed $25 million, a new revenue stream, to help companies develop trailblazing products and services. Already ten companies have pitched ideas, including a device to lower risk in laparoscopic surgery and a wearable monitor to better track patients' vitals. Four have been selected to reach the finals, where we begin the concept of commercializing the idea."

While the benefits of technology are numerous, they also require a new set of skills that all sectors need to master. For example, consider providers who need to master the electronic health record. While intended to create efficiencies, it also reduces the personal connection many providers prefer with their patients and vice versa. Providers often complain about the technical glitches and inefficiencies, such as interrupted system access, requiring them to create work-arounds that cause further increased burdens on their time.

The Rise of Consumerism

While there are far more than four significant challenges affecting the health industry, the last tsunami we will discuss is consumerism and its impact on the health industry. Direct-to-consumer advertising by pharmaceutical companies, payers, and health systems, as well as the near-ubiquity of the internet, have made it easy for consumers to obtain information about their medical conditions and possible treatments, making them informed and educated consumers.

The impact of consumerism on the industry is far-reaching. Consumers today prefer to partner with doctors than to rely on them passively to make treatment decisions. For drug manufacturers, consumers are challenging the return on investment for treatments, weighing the benefits against the costs. For insurers, consumers are challenging the cost of coverage and increasingly seeking alternative ways to access care at reduced cost. Consequently, all sectors of the industry are paying close attention to educating their consumers.

Carman Ciervo, DO, FACOFP, executive vice president and chief physician executive at Jefferson Health New Jersey, a regional health system, discusses a community-based initiative his organization led to better educate the population:

> One of our very successful initiatives was with ShopRite, a major supermarket in New Jersey. Their workforce is comprised of a diverse employee population with a variety of age groups, and we provided educational sessions

that addressed the health needs of those different groups. For example, we'd educate adults aged 40–50 about the appropriate screenings for their stage of life. Through this initiative, we learned that many of these people didn't have a primary care provider.

In addition to providing ShopRite's 1,200 employees with healthcare education, we were also able to connect them with primary care providers and access to healthcare. One employee we provided care to discovered she had chronic lymphocytic leukemia, and it's truly a success story, because we were able to detect it and treat it. After that, she became a strong advocate for our services and spread the word.

Getting into the community is how you begin to develop the trust that I feel creates the conditions for the success of your organization's population health initiatives.

All sectors will need to leverage online resources to improve the patient experience. Payers, providers, and pharmaceutical companies may be able to accelerate consumer engagement by developing online information resources, mobile applications, and personal health devices that can help consumers become more engaged.

Some large health systems are also using online resources as a response to the need for more transparency, recognizing that embracing openness as a core principle can differentiate them from competitors. Consumers also display a growing interest in electronic communication with providers.

The bottom line is that leveraging technology as part of personalized care will be one of the critical success factors for health organizations. The proliferation of easily available information related to health costs, conditions, testing options, and treatments means that patients are likely to be increasingly involved, alongside their clinicians, in medical decision-making.

KEY TAKEAWAYS

- Health status is most substantially affected by social determinants—controllable factors such as where we live, our physical environment, income, education level, diet, alcohol and substance use, and interpersonal relationships.
- As the industry shifts to payment models that incent for value, leaders will need to develop expertise in new areas of healthcare and shift to programs and services that reduce costs while enhancing quality outcomes.
- The four tsunamis of the health industry (payment reform, big data, technology, the rise of consumerism) are driving massive change in the ways various sectors connect with their customers.

REFERENCES

Centers for Medicare & Medicaid Services. 2018. "NHE Fact Sheet." Updated April 17. www.cms.gov/research-statistics-data-and -systems/statistics-trends-and-reports/nationalhealthexpend data/nhe-fact-sheet.html.

HCL. 2011. "Empowering the New Healthcare System." *HCL Technologies Press*.

Heiman, H. J., and S. Artiga. 2015. "Beyond Health Care: The Role of Social Determinants in Promoting Health and Health Equity." Allies for Reaching Community Health Equity. Published November 4. https://healthequity.globalpolicysolutions .org/resources/reports-and-fact-sheets/beyond-health-care-the -role-of-social-determinants-in-promoting-health-and-health -equity/.

Hussein, T., and M. Collins. 2016. "Why Big Health Systems Are Investing in Community Health." *Harvard Business*

Review. Published December 6. https://hbr.org/2016/12 /why-big-health-systems-are-investing-in-community-health.

Morrison, I. 2017. "Taking on the Social Determinants of Health." *H&HN*. Published October 24. www.hhnmag.com/articles.

CHAPTER 3

The Challenge of Collaboration

Alone we can do so little; together we can do so much.

—Helen Keller (quoted by Joseph P. Lash), 1980

A NEED THAT CAN'T BE IGNORED

The Center for Healthcare Governance (2016) suggests that hospitals and health systems should serve as "anchor institutions" and play a vital role as conveners, integrators, and facilitators of community partnerships. Our research firmly endorses this view and expands it to illustrate the need for *all* organizations across the health industry to play a vital role in forming community collaborations.

Fragmentation among the various stakeholders and the resulting lack of alignment is a significant obstacle to achieving demonstrable change in the health of our communities. Working collectively, executives need to drive the creation of new organizational models that leverage scale, expand expertise, share risk, and support the innovation required to improve population health. We are not alone in such thinking; the need to collaborate across sectors is already being recognized by players from across the health ecosystem.

To determine the latest views on working across the ecosystem, we surveyed 120 leaders from multiple health industry sectors. More than 80 percent of the leaders who responded to our survey saw external collaboration as important or very important to achieving their strategic objectives, noting that collaboration can enhance population health and enable better responses to the emerging payment models, as well as improve both access and quality. While collaboration is a great opportunity, the leadership challenges are significant, as authors Brian Williams, Vaughn Kauffman, and Karen Young (2017, 1) confirm:

> It's always a challenge for companies with divergent interests to coordinate services. But it's particularly hard to do so in healthcare—with its objective of the maintenance of human beings—as compared with, say, the maintenance of machinery in vehicles. Keeping a patient healthy requires addressing multiple systems.
>
> External factors such as diet, exercise, sleep, stress, and pollutants affect health. To try to predict the kinds of illnesses and conditions a person will suffer, and the kind of care they will need, an organization would need to consider a broad, complex data set that is meaningful at both the individual and the population level.

THE OLD WAYS OF WORKING ARE GONE

Collaboration introduces great complexity in defining working agreements and financial models, as well as effective policies, processes, and practices. This complexity, in turn, places a high demand on effective leadership to successfully navigate these uncharted waters.

While collaboration is recognized as important, the complexity and time frame required to build cross-sector relationships dissuades many organizations from pursuing these solutions. Firm commitment and leadership from the top are needed to generate agreement on how leaders will engage in the process and develop the ability to execute such a plan.

Issues will continually arise as collaboration efforts encounter emerging challenges, unexpected problems, and the inevitable failures that occur when uncharted territory is explored. Leaders with the right capabilities will create the conditions for success, and their mind-set and behavior will determine whether efforts continue or are terminated before reaching objectives. As scholar Amy C. Edmondson (2011) stated, the wisdom of learning from failing is incontrovertible, and when delving into new territory, failure should be embraced—it's the only road to improvement. The key challenge is to keep moving forward in a way that respects differences and manages tensions, attempts new solutions, and learns and adapts with a strong focus on purpose and opportunity. Leaders working across the ecosystem need the capability to manage the ongoing, inevitable strains that occur when stakeholders with differing views and backgrounds come together.

Solutions to challenges such as how reimbursement will be managed or how data will be shared are very complex. Our view is that the most significant obstacles to solving these "hard" problems will be the "soft" political, cultural, and interpersonal issues organizations will face as they begin to develop solutions to those recognized problems. Organizations that are part of our body of research recognize that leadership behavior affects internal cultures. When leaders demonstrate the right behaviors, their modeling greatly influences the organization's ability to meet external challenges.

Poonam Alaigh, MD, MSHCPM, FACP, former undersecretary for the US Department of Veterans Affairs, a federal agency that provides near-comprehensive healthcare services to military veterans, confirms the importance of leveraging soft skills to support collaboration:

> For collaboration to be successful, first you must show people that you care about them. When people come from different perspectives or vantage points, they are often siloed and come to the table with certain notions and patterns of thinking.
>
> If you're able to demonstrate that you care about them and the way they approach the issue, then the walls start to break down, trust builds, and you can have an honest

and transparent dialogue without concern for judgment. Building that foundation of trust where the stakeholders show they care for each other and are not dismissive of each other is critical.

BIGGER AND BROADER CHALLENGES

Collaboration requires organizations to invest in new capabilities, leverage resources, adopt new policies and practices, and develop and execute new processes and structures. Agreeing on financial incentives and levels of resources are also cited in our research as major challenges to developing and maintaining these collaborative solutions.

While these challenges affect organizations as they work across their departments, between geographies, and between the central organization and the operating units, problems are multiplied when organizations with different values, priorities, and perspectives need to work together. When uncharted territory is explored, collaboration efforts will encounter many challenges and unexpected problems, and initial failures are common. However, these issues can be overcome with the right mind-set. Here is Mohamed Diab, MD, former vice president of Provider Transformation at Aetna, a healthcare insurance company headquartered in Connecticut. He describes his method for aligning processes between his organization and its provider partners as it developed a joint venture relationship with Banner Health, a nonprofit health system operating 28 hospitals and specialty care clinics across 6 states.

> Our process is to look at the capabilities of each organization and collectively decide which services will be provided by each organization. When you bring two large organizations together around a common mission, it takes a lot of time to truly grasp the concept and understand what each organization is going to bring to the table.

It's an arduous process where every area of the organization is involved in the discussion—finance, compliance, regulatory, legal, pharmacy, medical management, etc. It can take at least 18 months of detailed negotiations and capability comparisons to determine what the infrastructure will look like.

As an illustrative example, Banner had a robust specialty pharmacy capability, and, as a major cost driver, it made more sense to delegate specialty pharmacy to Banner because it's part of the clinically integrated network. Aetna would complement that with wraparound services around local capabilities.

We can learn so much from these experiences. Behaviors such as self-interest and skepticism are the enemies in the process of leading across the health ecosystem. Organizations must examine, disclose, discuss, and manage their motivations. It is critical to the process that the leadership style encourages dialogue and allows conflict to surface and then be productively resolved.

CORE FACTORS FOR SUCCESS

Our research enabled us to develop a number of guideposts for how leaders need to work in the ecosystem to ensure the success of cross-sector collaboration. These are explored in more detail in the chapters to come; for now, we present the following findings:

1. Leading across the health ecosystem requires leaders to balance and leverage expectations, needs, resources, and contributions across sectors.
2. The ecosystem leader needs to be able to
   - create a compelling vision for her organization in the health ecosystem;

- engage a diverse set of stakeholders toward a broader vision and objectives;
- build and align internal and external systems, processes, and programs to provide the best quality and value while improving the health of the population;
- identify, develop, and optimize partnerships, collaborations, and organizational models that achieve the objectives for the population and meet the needs of the organization; and
- build the capacity of employees to lead and execute the strategy.

3. The leaders also need to create an environment of success that
   - aligns interests and guiding purpose across the stakeholders;
   - recognizes interdependence and the value the different parties contribute to the overall objectives;
   - stays focused on the right results, optimizing patient and population health;
   - allows for open and direct stakeholder dialogue;
   - clarifies stakeholder roles, establishes clear rules of engagement, and defines the decision-making process.

While many leaders demonstrate these capabilities working in their own organizations (cross-department, cross-function, cross-geography, cross–operating units), they need to recognize and prepare for the complexity that is multiplied when working across organizations with different purposes, cultures, values, governance, structures, metrics, and reward systems. The complexity of these efforts is described by Deloitte (2017) as follows:

- Having the right team with the right skills is critical, and engagement and buy-in must come from the top. CEO support and participation are necessary for collaboratives to endure.

- Success doesn't happen overnight. Patience, persistence, flexibility, and a long-term vision are essential.
- Strong collaboratives are dynamic. Many begin with one set of goals that shift over time.
- Cost savings are important, but achieving value or return on investment . . . from a provider collaborative extends to strengthening relationships, learning best practices, gaining clinical improvements, and creating a unified, more powerful voice.
- Collaborative members value the relationships they've built and see them as a defense strategy against future challenges in the changing healthcare market.

Leaders who demonstrate these capabilities build an environment that supports interpersonal trust, mutual respect, innovative thinking, and continuous learning. They confront the complex challenges inherent in working across the ecosystem, and, having done so, are positioned to build models and approaches that can improve affordability and the health of the communities in which they work.

KEY TAKEAWAYS

- All organizations across the health ecosystem need to play a vital role in forming community collaborations by serving as conveners, integrators, and facilitators of community partnerships.
- Leaders working across the ecosystem need to effectively manage the ongoing, inevitable tensions that occur when stakeholders with differing views and backgrounds come together.

- The key leadership challenge is to keep the conversation moving forward in a way that respects differences, attempts new solutions, and focuses on purpose and opportunity.
- To build successful cross-sector collaborations, leaders need to do the following:
  - Balance and leverage expectations, needs, resources, and contributions
  - Inspire and engage around a shared vision and develop key partnerships
  - Build and encourage employee innovation
  - Recognize interdependence
  - Focus on the right results
  - Foster a psychologically safe environment
  - Clarify roles and rules of engagement

REFERENCES

Center for Healthcare Governance. 2016. *Learnings on Governance from Partnerships That Improve Community Health*. American Hospital Association. Published February. http://trustees.aha.org/populationhealth/16-BRP-Learnings-on-Governance.pdf.

Deloitte. 2017. "Provider Collaboratives: Working Together to Navigate the Changing Healthcare Delivery System." *Modern Healthcare*. Accessed May 17, 2018. www.modernhealthcare.com/article/20170224/SPONSORED/170229954.

Edmondson, A. C. 2011. "Strategies for Learning from Failure." *Harvard Business Review*. Published April. www.hbr.org/2011/04/strategies-for-learning-from-failure.

Williams, B., V. Kauffman, and K. Young. 2017. "How Teamwork Will Transform Healthcare." *strategy+business*. Published August 21. www.strategy-business.com/article/How-Teamwork-Will-Transform-Healthcare.

CHAPTER 4

The New Health Ecosystem Leader

Leadership is the capacity to translate vision into reality.

—Warren Bennis, quoted by Dianna Daniels Booher, 1991

NEW STRATEGIES REQUIRE NEW LEADERSHIP CAPABILITIES

Before we present our health ecosystem leadership model (HELM), allow us to expand further on what leaders must do to meet the challenges of today's health ecosystem. To set the scene, here is Matthew Guy, MPA, senior consultant and coach at ReThink Health, a national health strategy consulting firm committed to convening cross-sector collaborative solutions:

> The culture of collaboration needs to be demonstrated from the top, so it can cascade down to the lower levels of the organization. Leaders must bring people in from other organizations, or even other industries, and have them talk about what they're doing to create links between what the respective organizations are doing.
>
> Executives must show all their leaders how the organization fits into the broader context of the health ecosystem and the impact the organization has on the system. The

problem most senior leaders have is that they try to force their ideals down the throats of whomever they are trying to get to cooperate.

Rather than trying to transform everyone's entire view about how things are done in the organization, just try to get them to understand the organization's role in the larger scheme of the health ecosystem and how their work fits into this broader context.

Effective leadership has always included a broad array of skills, behaviors, and competencies including change leadership, innovation, and negotiation. While these competencies remain wholly important, what we've uncovered through our work with organizations across the health ecosystem is a new set of competencies for effective cross-sector collaboration, and a new context in which existing competencies need to be applied. If you're a leader who believes in the need for an ecosystem approach to realize improvements in your organization, your sector, and across sectors, then the leadership model and mind-set apply to you.

The health ecosystem is certainly complex. Made up of powerful players with disparate interests, it is nested in larger societal, market, and governance systems of even greater complexity, with traditional approaches to strategy design being solely industry focused and organizationally executed. To develop ecosystem solutions, organizations need to think much more broadly, inviting other sectors and diverse perspectives to the strategic planning table. Craig Samitt, currently of Blue Cross and Blue Shield and formerly of Anthem, endorsed this point when he told us that

Things have gotten very complex, and there is an absence of an entity that has "stepped up" to bring order out of chaos. As things become more complex, there's a greater need for order. I think now is the time for us to step forward with a new set of solutions.

This new set of solutions will require competing management teams and boards to come together under the shared goal of improving population health. Each sector brings its unique strength to the shared goal and offers relevant best practices to derive the greatest value from the group's collective efforts.

Sometimes, these organizations will not be direct competitors but potential allies that, though they occupy different sectors, have the opportunity to work together to improve overall health. For example, we are aware of providers working with a housing authority, a utility company, and a food bank. Such is the extent of this new world.

Complementary sectors—and competing ones—codesigning a collective and collaborative strategy will ensure that the conditions are set so that ecosystem solutions can be implemented with proper alignment and engagement across all important players. For success to be confidently achieved, such initiatives require enough leaders with the right capabilities in place to support the new strategies.

THE OLD BOUNDARIES AND BORDERS ARE GONE

Leaders who will be successful in this new world understand the importance of collaboration—whether it's with other leaders in their organization or with potential partner organizations—and also recognize that it will be difficult. They accept that the isolation of leaders in their own worlds (whether in their particular organization or their health industry sector) can create bias, and they also know that the way to move forward is to find opportunities to align around common interests while not being derailed by differences. These visionaries walk into the room with the goal of finding common ground, seeking to create an environment in which people can explore different solutions without passing judgment. They take the time to truly understand how and why the other party approaches a particular situation in a certain way.

One of the things we have learned from our research is that ecosystem development activities take time, often competing with the day-to-day operations of the organization. As a result, the collaboration work can get less attention than needed—or in some cases efforts are abandoned. Leaders operating effectively across their ecosystem understand the need to take the time to look for ways in which their differing approaches serve their important common interests.

Successful collaboration requires leaders who are willing to step outside of the context that they typically operate in, to expand the solution space and invite others into the conversation, giving them ample opportunity to participate in developing solutions. For example, bold strategies—such as the Institute for Healthcare Improvement's Triple Aim for improving the care experience and overall health, as well as reducing costs, require leaders to work across sectors, particularly in the areas of population health and affordability. This task is not easy.

The Triple Aim, and other important efforts to improve health and affordability, are not congruent with the current business models of many US health organizations. Their traditional approach is focused on enhancing revenue and managing expenses to produce profits. They are driven by their mission statements and strategies, the focus on their customers, and which of their organizational capabilities can meet the needs of those customers. For organizations to be successful at efforts such as the Triple Aim, they need to bridge those differences. You can't have the hospitals lose if you are a payer, you can't have the payers lose if you are a hospital, and that means finding a formula that allows everyone to achieve common goals collectively.

Bridging these differences requires leadership in an environment in which there is no line of authority, goals are more diverse, business models are more variable, and culture and values are different from sector to sector. It starts with leaders saying, "You know what? Ultimately this a zero-sum game, and I don't think we can let anybody lose."

THE NEW TYPE OF LEADER

The bottom line is that the right leaders need to be in place to drive an ecosystem strategy forward and to take on the myriad challenges that come with it. This critical role of leadership is endorsed by Tsun-Yan Hsieh and Sara Yik (2005, 1): "Since bold strategies often require breakthroughs along a number of fronts, a company needs stronger and more dominant leadership at all levels if these strategies are to succeed."

We wrote this book because we think it's critical that health organizations have leaders with the capacity to think and behave in ways that support ecosystem solutions. Our research presents examples of leaders that have taken that wider view on specific problems, with a corresponding improvement in population health. These are cases where leaders have looked beyond their borders and connected with others in different sectors to address some of the much broader determinants of health.

The leaders we have interviewed clearly demonstrate tangible benefits from both cost and outcome standpoints, and this improvement goes back to our envisioning statement of a new focus on health. However, we are citing some exceptional cases. Imagine what the health ecosystem could collectively achieve if all the sectors worked together as their way of doing business? How would that affect the overall health of our nation? How would that affect cost? How would that affect the quality of life?

Organizations are made up of people, and their cultures are created by the ways in which employees behave largely because of the signals they receive from the executives and senior leaders. To change the organization's culture, it's important to have leaders who recognize the vital need to operate differently and who are willing to put in the time and effort and persist through difficult challenges. Leaders who exhibit the right behaviors in ecosystem initiatives can shift the culture of their own organizations in new and better directions by demonstrating and communicating that collaboration is not just worth the effort, it's critical to the mission. A collaborative mind-set becomes embedded in the organization when leaders' decisions and actions visibly reflect the importance of working across the ecosystem.

To further improve health and provide more value for the health-care dollar, the decisions and actions of leaders need to reflect the broader mind-set of achieving change via cross-entity efforts. The more leaders think and operate in this way, the more contagious and natural it will become across organizations, sectors, and the health industry.

KEY TAKEAWAYS

- Leaders need to think more broadly about how their organizations fit into and affect the larger ecosystem and invite leaders from other sectors with diverse perspectives to the strategic planning table.
- Complementary sectors—and competing ones—need to be engaged in the codesign of collective and collaborative solutions to create the alignment needed for successful implementation of solutions.
- Ongoing tensions will inevitably occur when stakeholders with differing worldviews try to work together; leaders who balance these diverse perspectives and focus on achieving mutual goals will create greater value for patients and populations.
- Leaders who exhibit a collaborative mind-set can shift the culture of their own organizations in a new and better direction by demonstrating and communicating that collaboration is critical to their mission.

REFERENCE

Hsieh, T. Y., and S. Yik. 2005. "Leadership as the Starting Point
of Strategy." *McKinsey Quarterly*. Published February. www.
mckinsey.com/featured-insights/leadership/leadership
-as-the-starting-point-of-strategy.

CHAPTER 5

Leading for Collaborative Solutions

Collaboration is the essence of life. The wind, bees,
and flowers work together to spread the pollen.

—Amit Ray, 2015

FINDING YOUR WAY FORWARD

In chapter 2, we described the current state of the health industry as a perfect storm for change. If we loosely continue that analogy here, navigating the health ecosystem can be choppy, gusty, and, at times, outright treacherous. The ecosystem represents an ocean of well-marked beacons, but the currents running among them are uncharted. Bridging these sector divides is the core principle—the north star—of the health ecosystem leadership model (HELM).

While it is complex and difficult, an ecosystem approach is a critical path to improving value. We previously cited John Geraci (2016), who examines how organizations create new value and growth by forging new connections to solve problems. Those business improvements could not be created when working alone.

The health industry needs this kind of collaboration. The Robert Wood Johnson Foundation (2018, 1) comments on health and social issues: "If there is one notion that captures what is needed to create a Culture of Health, it is that existing boundary lines must be crossed. Whether it is the public and private sector, the health and social sectors, or the silos that exist within the healthcare system, a new culture requires combined efforts that remove the barriers that each has placed around its work."

Clearly, the range of players that must contribute to improving health, affordability, and value *must* extend beyond any individual sector of the health industry. Providers, payers, and pharmaceutical and other life science companies need to seek ways to work with entities within the broader social sector, such as community health organizations, government at all levels, community entities, schools, and others. Not only is extending collaboration into the social sector the right thing to do, it can be the smart business thing to do. Michael E. Porter and Mark R. Kramer (2011) argue that companies can move beyond corporate social responsibility and gain competitive advantage by including social and environmental considerations in their strategies. Treating societal challenges as business opportunities, they suggest, is the most important new dimension of corporate strategy and the most powerful path to social progress.

In our survey of health industry leaders, respondents were unanimous in saying that the primary external challenges facing their organizations were the changing nature of payment models, the shifting regulatory environment, and the increased intensity of competition. Those issues can be tackled when working across the ecosystem.

Collaboration can open doors to unforeseen solutions to these challenges, and, as we've discussed already, it also introduces great complexity. Defining working agreements and financial models, as well as effective policies, processes, and practices across organizations and sectors, is no easy task, and it places leaders firmly in uncharted waters. Our HELM model offers the necessary guidance to navigate these new situations successfully, so that new organizational relationships capable of achieving goals such as the Triple Aim can be effectively developed.

In today's world, health industry leaders are understandably focused on trying to keep their own organizations on track. However, we believe that continuing to focus on sustaining a health system characterized by silos, conflicts of interest, and an us-versus-them mentality will not produce viable long-term solutions for the health industry and is contrary to the shared goal of improved health.

We offer specific examples of leaders working together to create innovative solutions to complex issues—such as access, reimbursement, and data sharing—by leading across sectors. We believe that this new type of leader is vital in the industry today.

AN INTRODUCTION TO HELM

Developed by surveying and interviewing industry leaders across all sectors, HELM offers a complete framework for how leaders can behave to generate cross-sector solutions to the health industry's most pressing needs. Multiorganizational collaboration requires adoption of an ecosystem mind-set, commitment of time, development of trust, alignment on business priorities, and agreement regarding the value of collaboration. In essence, achievement of these goals needs the HELM approach.

As we'll explore in the pages to come, generating ecosystem solutions to solve complex health challenges is a dynamic and ever-evolving process. The model that we have developed is examined in detail in chapters 6 through 9. An overview of the model's four components and the leadership challenges HELM is designed to confront are outlined in the following sections.

Envision the Future

Leaders must have a clear vision of the direction their organization is heading and what it hopes to achieve. Once that vision is in place, they can begin to generate ideas about how collaborating with organizations from other sectors can contribute to achieving their goals. Thinking with an ecosystem view allows leaders to generate solutions they may not have otherwise considered.

Align Stakeholders

As organizations bring stakeholders from other sectors into the conversation, leaders must allow these stakeholders to build on their original vision and incorporate their inputs and interests to develop a shared solution. This exploration and dialogue allows all stakeholders to feel a sense of ownership of the solution.

Throughout these conversations, it is important to develop a relationship built on trust, respect, and open dialogue. Without that, tension can build up and be followed by resistance to moving forward.

Manage Boundaries and Obstacles

The path toward developing collaborative solutions will not be smooth. To overcome the inevitable obstacles, it's important that leaders focus on opportunity and remind themselves of why the partnership was developed initially. Difficult conversations are likely to occur throughout the process and cannot be avoided. Such dialogue allows stakeholders to resolve points of tension, clarify roles, and realign on ways the respective organizations can interface effectively.

Act and Learn

Leaders must take concrete steps toward advancing the shared vision that was created at the onset of the collaboration. This approach usually requires acting under uncertain conditions to address previously unseen challenges.

As actions are taken, some results will offer positive outcomes and others will be less successful. It is critical to be open to giving and receiving feedback so that any shortfalls may be leveraged to better meet the common objectives and needs of all stakeholders.

CONCLUSION

This HELM overview illustrates that developing effective cross-sector solutions is a journey that can be characterized as a sequence of actions. Outlined in a linear way, these actions are typically revisited and reworked at multiple points through the process of ecosystem collaboration. Successful leaders of the health ecosystem will span the boundaries between organizations and manage the ongoing tensions that characterize relationships between stakeholders with diverse values, perspectives, priorities, and incentives. This balance is what HELM is all about (see exhibit 5.1).

Leading effectively across the health ecosystem centers around new approaches and a new mind-set across all sectors of the health

Exhibit 5.1: Health Ecosystem Leadership Model (HELM)

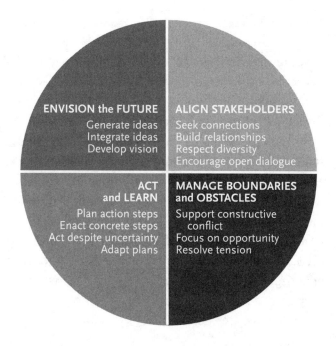

ENVISION the FUTURE
Generate ideas
Integrate ideas
Develop vision

ALIGN STAKEHOLDERS
Seek connections
Build relationships
Respect diversity
Encourage open dialogue

ACT and LEARN
Plan action steps
Enact concrete steps
Act despite uncertainty
Adapt plans

MANAGE BOUNDARIES and OBSTACLES
Support constructive conflict
Focus on opportunity
Resolve tension

industry. After all, to achieve better health at an affordable cost, new levels of collaboration and partnership between all sectors are required. Consider the following from the American Hospital Association and the American Medical Association (2015), who comment, "While challenges exist, they are not insurmountable when professionalism, respect, and cooperation are at the core of this partnership and when the vision is clear how best to meet the needs of their patients and communities that they are privileged to serve."

We agree that respect and collaboration between physicians and health systems, between executives within those systems and the payers who set pricing and control benefits, between health systems and the drug manufacturers who design treatments to control and treat diseases, and so on, with a shared focus on the needs of patients and communities, should be an expectation for those who lead our nation's health organizations.

KEY TAKEAWAYS

- Leading effectively across the health ecosystem is all about new approaches and a new mind-set across all sectors of the health industry.
- The health ecosystem leadership model (HELM) comprises four clusters: envisioning the future, aligning stakeholders, managing boundaries and obstacles, and acting and learning. These frame how leaders must behave to generate cross-sector solutions to the health industry's most pressing needs.
- Leaders who consistently demonstrate the behaviors in HELM will successfully span the boundaries between organizations and manage the ongoing tensions that characterize relationships between stakeholders with diverse values, perspectives, priorities, and incentives.

REFERENCES

American Hospital Association and American Medical Association. 2015. "Integrated Leadership for Hospitals and Health Systems: Principles for Success." *The Journal of the Oklahoma State Medical Association* 108 (5–6): 281–88.

Geraci, J. 2016. "How an Ecosystem Mindset Can Help People and Organizations Succeed." *Harvard Business Review*. Published May 12. www.hbr.org/2016/05/how-an-ecosystem-mindset -can-help-people-and-organizations-succeed.

Porter, M. E., and M. R. Kramer. 2011. "Creating Shared Value." *Harvard Business Review*. Published January–February. www.hbr .org/2011/01/the-big-idea-creating-shared-value.

Robert Wood Johnson Foundation. 2018. "Defining and Measuring a Culture of Health." Accessed February 22. www.rwjf.org/en /library/research/2016/10/defining-and-measuring-a-culture -of-health.html.

CHAPTER 6

Envision the Future

The leader has to be practical and a realist, yet must talk the language of the visionary and the idealist.

—Eric Hoffer, 1951

IN THEIR BOOK *Building the Future*, which looks at the founding of a smart city for broader leadership lessons, Amy C. Edmondson and Susan Salter Reynolds (2016, 10) propose that true innovation across boundaries—a requirement for the creation of such a city—starts with "building a shared vision that evolves as more is learned." Our work with some of the pioneers of collaboration in the health industry suggests that health ecosystem leadership begins in the same place.

Creating the vision of cross-sector collaboration in our industry is a dynamic process that begins with three leadership actions:

1. Generating what-if ideas
2. Iterating those initial ideas and integrating them with the ideas of others
3. Further developing a vision and creative ideas

In this chapter, we explore these actions and provide examples from ecosystem leaders who demonstrate these behaviors.

GENERATE WHAT-IF IDEAS AND SOLUTIONS TO ACHIEVE OPTIMAL GOALS

Today's truly effective health leaders recognize the need to work with others in their ecosystem. This need exists whether an opportunity is focused on broad issues, such as reducing the cost of care or improving the health of an overall population, or is about a more specific issue, such as reducing unnecessary emergency department (ED) visits.

Ecosystem leaders avoid jumping to immediate conclusions and quick-win solutions because they recognize that when these are established from a single sector perspective, they are unlikely to deliver the desired set of outcomes. Instead, these leaders begin by stepping back to consider a broad view, taking the time to consider the situation in its entirety. They postpone suggesting answers until they have defined the problem holistically. Then they look for the multiple factors that could be creating the challenge or that could contribute to potential solutions.

These leaders openly recognize that their approach is likely to be too heavily influenced by their own industry experience and organizational approaches. To avoid this bias, they proactively seek out views from other people, particularly those with different experience or expertise, who might see the problem differently. In regard to this need for a broad approach, David Carmouche of Ochsner notes, "The thing that stymies progress the most in the health industry is a lack of understanding of each other's business objectives, priorities, and challenges. It is amazing the misperceptions that have been generated over decades that still persist today that are just factually incorrect."

Ecosystem leaders look for parallel problems in other organizations, including competitors and organizations from other industry sectors, and try to understand the others' perspectives and the solutions they have attempted. What has worked for them? What has not? What do the successes have in common? What seem to be the solutions that are less successful?

To maximize the benefits of ecosystem collaboration, leaders must spend time understanding how customers and relevant groups in their community see things—they must be driven by a desire to understand perspectives from the other side of the fence. Often these efforts take the form of community needs assessments designed to generate answers to such questions as, What is the community's experience? What does it believe is working well? What is getting in its way?

On this matter, Barry Ostrowsky of RWJBarnabas Health notes:

> Efforts to enhance the health of the communities we serve is a huge undertaking, and this requires leaders to demonstrate an ecosystem view by focusing resources on understanding the needs of their community. To be successful, it's important to learn about these, as well as [about] your own organization's capacity in terms of resources and what has already been done.
>
> The needs of the community determine the types of social programs we can provide because one size won't fit all. For example, the needs in Newark are different from the needs in New Brunswick. They may be similar in that they are both vulnerable communities, but the same programs won't serve the needs of both.

Truly understanding the breadth of community needs is vital, and leaders working in accordance with the principles of the health ecosystem leadership model (HELM) actively encourage people in their own organizations to devote sufficient time and resources to gathering this information. For example, here's Julie Miller-Phipps, president of Kaiser Foundation Health Plan and Hospitals in Southern California: "We have a group that spends a lot of time on the phone with patients who are considered high risk to understand their social determinants and how their needs are contributing to the frequent health issues they're experiencing."

With prevention now in mind as much as cure has always been, all of these different and new perspectives contribute to a much broader and more complex picture of an ideal end state. What should the best customer experience look like? Who should be contributing to the solution? What would they be doing? Ecosystem leaders imagine solutions that collaboration across entities and sectors can make possible, and then they roll up their sleeves and lead from the front.

As with Julie Miller-Phipps's Kaiser group, this belief in the value of the ecosystem approach typically includes a strong focus on the social determinants of health. This emphasis broadens the view of any health problem or opportunity and is often the starting point for envisioning a different future for the system of health.

This ecosystem mind-set motivates leaders to think outside their traditional areas of focus. John Lloyd, co-CEO of Hackensack Meridian Health, recognizes that he must find a new way to conceptualize what it means to be a provider organization and how the importance of social determinants begins to drive the necessary change: "As a healthcare provider, we don't get paid to provide meals for patients. But if we're getting paid for the outcomes, and we don't want that person to be readmitted, we need to begin to think differently about where our role in care delivery really ends. As a health system, we need to be paying attention to the social determinants because it allows us to approach patient care from a holistic point of view rather than just focusing on clinical care."

ITERATE IDEAS AND INTEGRATE THEM WITH THE THINKING OF OTHERS

HELM leaders recognize that their initial ideas and vision are only the beginning. As other perspectives are solicited, they actively listen to and acknowledge the views and concerns of the other health industry leaders and representatives from their ecosystem communities.

Many of these other stakeholders will have also spent time thinking about and working on the identified issue and will have their own ideas. It is critical that these perspectives are heard and are used to further inform the overall vision of what is truly possible. Bob Hemker, retired president and CEO of Palomar Health, provides this example of how his organization sought to learn about the methods other stakeholders have used to tackle an issue and apply the learning to Palomar's own community:

> The county of San Diego has been challenged with insufficient behavioral health capacity, leading to an inordinate amount of holds in the system where the patients are potentially in the ED for days awaiting placement into a care facility.
>
> We sought a new model of care for behavioral health, and one of our executives had a connection at Alameda County who was running a program to implement a crisis stabilization unit (CSU). They allowed us to make site visits to better understand their model programmatically.
>
> Crisis stabilization is designed as a targeted 24-hour program to stabilize the patient in the right venue of care and return them to their normal situation. If they are unable to be stabilized, then their care would be escalated to an inpatient setting.
>
> We collaborated with San Diego County to be one of their pilot sites as a CSU. In doing so, we were able to reduce the strain on our ED and provide better care in a more appropriate and cost-effective setting.

It is exciting to note that in more and more communities and organizations, mechanisms are being put in place to create and execute a truly shared vision. Donna Mills, executive director of the Central Oregon Health Council, a not-for-profit community governance entity, describes the work of the diverse group that she leads:

> The council's board is made up of stakeholders from healthcare providers, local governments, educators, community-based and nonprofit organizations, and other

entities in the region. Our board is responsible for creating a regional health improvement plan as a long-term, systematic effort to address public health problems on the basis of the results of health assessment activities and the health improvement process.

Through working together, the improvement plan defines the vision for the health of the community through a collaborative process and offers strategies to improve the health status of that community.

DEVELOP AND ADVANCE A VISION AND CREATIVE SOLUTIONS

Ecosystem leaders are confident in what they are trying to achieve and are prepared to share their perspectives with others. HELM leaders take the time to understand others and not prematurely judge. Listening to your peers is an important step, but it is not enough. As new perspectives are offered, building and advancing a future vision requires leaders to examine their own assumptions continuously and be open to modifying those attitudes. The new vision created must be meaningful, engaging, and adaptable in the best interests of all those who have a place at the collaboration table.

While the initial future vision may be drafted for a given organization, it needs to address the views that multiple stakeholders recognize as important. At the appropriate time, stakeholders in the community who can contribute to the opportunity are identified and invited to participate in defining potential solutions. Leaders with the right approach to ecosystem thinking will be as willing to join others who initiate a program of change as they are to drive their own initiatives. Recall the employment boot camp program that Barry Ostrowsky of RWJBarnabas Health described in chapter 2. He and his organization were not alone in the mission to address unemployment as a critical social determinant in the community.

At the same time as we were developing our Hire Newark program, the mayor informed me of his vision, called *Newark 2020*. The objective of his vision was to increase economic development by the year 2020 in the hiring of 2,020 unemployed Newark residents and enlisting the participation of the significant organizations in the city, both for-profit and not-for-profit.

Not only did I volunteer my organization to be part of his vision, but I also took on the leadership role of contacting the CEOs of other major organizations in Newark and enlisted buy-in from PSE&G, Prudential, Horizon Blue Cross, and other organizations that have long been committed to the welfare of Newark.

I invited these organizations to the table and said that we want to expand our mission through collaboration because we think we can lead a better approach to improving the lives of the people in our community by working together.

I'm happy to say that it's resonated, because they, too, had a preexisting disposition toward helping the city. The mayor's vision simply gave us all an effective vehicle to do so, and we are beginning to see real activity along those lines.

Barry is talking about rallying support beyond his healthcare boundaries because joining one's vision and perspectives with those of others can offer the opportunity to create a unified view of the future that can have even more impact. He did not seek to be in competition with the mayor but to join forces.

This gathering of others brings us nicely to our more detailed look at the second cluster of HELM: aligning stakeholders. Effective ecosystem collaboration is not limited only to identifying the ideal players—it includes taking very specific and effective steps to ensure that all players understand and buy into a shared purpose for the collaboration initiative.

KEY TAKEAWAYS

- Envisioning the future of cross-sector collaboration in the health industry is a dynamic process that begins with three leadership actions:
  1. *Generating what-if ideas and solutions to achieve optimal goals* involves leaders seeking out views from other people and not jumping to immediate conclusions.
  2. *Iterating those initial ideas and integrating them with the ideas of others* requires soliciting and actively listening to what is said while acknowledging the views and concerns of other participants in an ecosystem community.
  3. *Developing and advancing a vision and creative ideas* requires leaders to continuously examine their own assumptions and be open to modifying those assumptions to ensure that the vision is meaningful, engaging, and adaptable to all who have a place at the collaboration table.
- Leaders who demonstrate ecosystem thinking embrace opportunities to align with other efforts focused on similar objectives.
- Actively encouraging and devoting time and resources to gathering information to understand the needs in the communities will contribute to a more comprehensive picture of an ideal end state.

REFERENCE

Edmondson, A. C., and S. Salter Reynolds. 2016. *Building the Future: Big Teaming for Audacious Innovation.* Oakland, CA: Berrett-Koehler Publishers.

CHAPTER 7

Align Stakeholders

*The best way to lead people into the future is to
connect with them deeply in the present.*

—James M. Kouzes and Barry Posner, 2009

IN THE PROCESS of envisioning the future, ecosystem leaders take
the time to look to others to help inform a collective vision. To
continue to move those ideals forward, they need to actively engage
other leaders—beyond their organization and sector—to ensure
that everyone is "singing from the same song sheet." It is critical to
bring together all stakeholders who have, or could certainly develop,
a vested interest in the vision of the collaboration initiative and get
them working together effectively.

These people see the potential to build cross-sector solutions,
and, together, they discuss and further develop the ideas, mutually
determining how best they can all cooperate with each other. To
demonstrate this point, Matthew Guy of ReThink Health describes
a situation in which his organization convened different stakeholder
groups to work collaboratively:

> In my role at ReThink Health, I act as a facilitator of orga-
> nizations who want to change health outcomes from a
> systemic perspective rather than from their individual silo

or even their industry silo. A good example comes from some of the work we're doing in New Mexico.

Presbyterian Health System (the largest health system in Albuquerque) and University of New Mexico Health System were the original actors that we interviewed, and they were willing to come to the table to talk. Presbyterian Health System is a combined payer and provider but was very interested in involving a large payer *outside* of Presbyterian.

We were fortunate to have some conversations with New Mexico Health Connections, New Mexico's health insurance co-op. When we approached the CEO, Martin Hickey, he was very interested in our work and how it would impact the work of the co-op.

We were able to enlist buy-in from him for this collaboration because he believed in the need for integration and connection with other parts of the healthcare system, not just by being a payer but even getting involved in delivery as well.

Because he believed in the importance of change in the health ecosystem in a broader sense and the value of different actors working together, we brought these organizations together to discuss collaboration solutions.

In this stage of building ecosystem solutions, consistent with the health ecosystem leadership model (HELM) approach, conversations continue to focus on understanding multiple perspectives and learning about diverse sets of expertise that exist across the sectors. The focus is on where the individual and collective strengths lie so that these can be leveraged for maximum benefit for the common cause.

As the participants each share their views on the opportunity and present activities they are undertaking that are related to it, each needs to carefully listen to *all* the ideas and perspectives being shared. The nature of the opportunity is explored and iterated, areas of focus are agreed on, and potential solutions are identified and reviewed.

While the players around the table may have been motivated to work together based on their own needs, ecosystem leaders remain mindful of what has brought them to take part in the collaborative. Jeffrey Le Benger, MD, board chair and CEO of Summit Medical Group, a multispecialty physician group in New Jersey, endorses the point that good collaborations come from the right leaders (Knowles 2018, 4): "A group has to have the right culture to be able to make a quality partnership. When evaluating whether a potential partner is a good fit, I first look at their leadership team and how they think. You may laugh at this, but I look at their body language. I look at how they talk and the culture of the group. It always starts from the top." Once people have been brought together, dialogue is the tool that builds and strengthens relationships, allowing the diverse players to work through the inevitable tensions that will arise. Ultimately, to move forward, the stakeholders must work to align around a common purpose, objectives, and areas of focus.

Aligning stakeholders requires leaders to do the following:

- Seek connections with others to further a broad purpose
- Take concrete steps to enable the group to come together effectively and build relationships
- Demonstrate respect for a diversity of expertise, perspectives, interests, and values
- Encourage open dialogue and exchange of interests, ideas, expertise, and information across stakeholders

Let's look at each of these actions more closely.

SEEK CONNECTIONS WITH OTHERS TO FURTHER A BROAD PURPOSE

In envisioning the future, the initiating leader has created a picture of a solution that could be possible if the right set of stakeholders come together. Now it is time to explicitly identify and reach out to the groups and sectors who were seen as potential contributors to the solution. At this stage in the process, as ecosystem leaders actively connect with other stakeholders for the first time, they know that new players often contribute in ways that shift the vision toward a different direction. Being open to other possibilities allows for creativity and innovative thinking. It is certainly not uncommon, and often desirable, to redefine the vision after new stakeholders are added to the process.

Thus, while they confidently share their vision, health ecosystem leaders are careful not to overstate their position. They fully expect that the vision will evolve as each stakeholder contributes her ideas and the leader "in the chair" actively seeks contributions to the vision from all parties. These leaders know that when all stakeholders have an opportunity to build a shared vision and purpose, the emerging solutions are more likely to make it through the potential turbulence ahead.

Tanisha Carino, PhD, former vice president of US Public Policy at GlaxoSmithKline (a pharmaceutical company headquartered in London), is a great example of an ecosystem leader who looked beyond the four walls of her own organization to seek connections with organizations with a shared purpose. In her words,

> We recognized that America's Health Insurance Plans has existing proposals around improving adult immunization, so we approached those who spearheaded that work about collaborating to continue advancing their efforts. While our respective companies may differ on some issues, we clearly share common ground on other issues—namely adult immunization rates.
>
> We pulled together a small group of sponsors and identified other influential thought leaders who we believed needed to be part of the discussion. It was challenging to get all of these key people in the same room at the same time, but we were able to dedicate a half-day meeting where we identified specific policy solutions to advance.

As Tanisha demonstrates, ecosystem leaders take the time to consider the views of other stakeholders and their businesses. Followers of HELM recognize that what works for them may not work for the other stakeholders and that each participant in an ecosystem collaboration might have a different preferred approach.

That means that finding common ground is essential, as demonstrated by Lorie Shoemaker, senior vice president and chief nursing officer at Catholic Health Initiatives, Texas Division:

> The reason people go into medicine—whether you become an administrator, physician, nurse, etc.—is with the patient or consumer at the center. That's our common denominator. As long as we can focus on what's in the best interest of the patient, we can at least get people to the table. It sounds simple, but you've got to break down a whole lot of barriers to get there. The more stakeholders there are around the table, the more personalities and competing interests there are to align.
>
> I start any big project by clearly identifying the vision. We have to agree on what we're trying to accomplish, and then every meeting and every decision is made with the underlying question in mind, "How does this further our mission and vision?" If you don't align on the vision at the get-go, you will struggle throughout the whole process. Your decisions will be faulty, and you'll be regrouping constantly.

Because people differ in terms of how they prefer to receive information, such as headlines versus details or leading with the bottom line versus building up to your conclusion, ecosystem leaders take the time to understand these preferences and shape their communications to fit the preferred style of each stakeholder. They make sure they are not moving too fast or too far ahead of others, and they focus on problem definition and all of its elements before sharing any potential solutions.

A great technique to drive engagement and aid shared understanding is to use stories to help make the identified opportunity feel real and compelling. Whether from personal experience or popular culture, practical examples are used to illustrate real people, facing real problems, benefiting from creative solutions. Julie Miller-Phipps of Kaiser Permanente in Southern California provides a great example:

> To get others engaged in collaboration, as often as I can, I align the "ask" with my personal story. For example, in Orange County, I worked on a project dedicated to helping disenfranchised young adults get on a better track in their lives. We were charged with engaging companies in the community to offer mentorship programs for the most vulnerable population.
>
> I brought the issue back to my department managers and met with them on a routine basis to educate them about the community need and the support required by Kaiser. I shared my own personal story about being one of the first to graduate in my family and engaged them in a conversation by asking how many of them were first-time graduates in their families. This created conversation about what it took for them to overcome the barriers to achieving their goals. At the end of the conversation, I asked for volunteers who would be willing to mentor an individual over a 6-month period—I had 40 people raise their hands.
>
> I took that list of people back to the project board and talked to the CEOs around the room about the process I had gone through to engage these people. It was a tremendous source of pride for me that I could engage with our people and have them so readily volunteer for such a worthwhile endeavor.

TAKE CONCRETE STEPS TO ENABLE THE GROUP TO COME TOGETHER AND BUILD RELATIONSHIPS

Because strong relationships are so important for building and implementing ecosystem solutions, leaders driving a collaborative initiative ensure enough time is set aside for people to get to know each other. This familiarity helps build trust and makes it more likely that stakeholders will give each other the benefit of the doubt when tensions arise.

Logistically, bringing various stakeholders together is often one of the biggest challenges. However, getting the right people around the table from the outset is extremely valuable. What is required of the stakeholders is to be open and willing to listen and seek others in the group to be open and willing to listen.

Stakeholders also need to be capable of creating the space to do the work. Competing time commitments are real. Exploring how the group can minimize time conflicts while maximizing benefits in the shortest possible time is as important as having the right people around the table. Furthermore, establishing the right setting and atmosphere is imperative.

Again, here's Lorie Shoemaker from Catholic Health Initiatives, Texas Division, speaking about how the facilitator needs to adapt and change—reflecting on what we said earlier about people's different information needs—in order to drive the right outcomes in stakeholder alignment:

> At first, we held a series of one-off meetings to just get the ball rolling. Then, we held a two-day retreat to bring all these stakeholders together. Everyone at that retreat was an innovative thinker, allowing us to freely share our priorities and imperatives. There were several brainstorming sessions that eventually resulted in a project plan for what became an unbelievable program.

In leading such initiatives, I have had to learn to develop patience with the process. I'm a critical care nurse by background, and so I've spent many years taking care of the sickest of the sick. It is my nature and inclination to make decisions with the best available information that I have, and I've had to make these decisions quickly because patients' lives depend on it. I've had to learn that not everybody thinks like that; some people are much more data driven and need more information and time to make a decision.

I've also had to learn to slow down and let people process what is being discussed. But at the end of the day, we have to keep pushing forward. I give people enough time to process but give them a fixed end point, so that a decision can be made and we can move on to accomplish our overall goal.

As Lorie suggests, while conversations continue, leaders must monitor the pace and amount of information being shared to ensure it is not too much, too soon, for the other stakeholders. This prudence is particularly important in early conversations with people the leader may not know well, and again, leaders must be open in their thinking.

Those who lead in the ecosystem help others to understand how to mutually approach work, problems, or opportunities. Everyone is encouraged to share the assumptions that shape their perspectives, and they talk openly about things they ruled out and why. This transparency helps others in the group to know each other better—especially the leader, who models the desirable behaviors and thus increases the willingness of others to share.

To underscore this point, Josh Ofman from Amgen describes how his organization gained the trust of a potential collaborative partner through openness and transparency:

We recently sent out a press release about a three-year collaborative partnership with Humana, one of the largest payers in the country. Humana was a very logical partner because we have a shared interest in population health. They have always been a leader in public health and have an organization within Humana that is focused on how to measure and collect data in the populations they serve. All those things together made them a terrific choice for a potential partnership, and we reached out to their senior leadership team to discuss opportunities to work together.

As you may know, there's a lot of skepticism from payers about our industry's motives. We had to work to gain their trust, so that they could recognize our sincere intention of identifying mutual areas of interest. The first thing we did was pull together a small group of executives to open up the conversation and get to know one another. We had to be sure to have the right people around the table and be very transparent to demonstrate our mind-set of collaboration.

Once we broke through that initial barrier of getting to know each other's points of view and aligning on mutual goals, we held a series of subsequent meetings to begin generating creative ideas and fleshing them out. We are now working with them on several different projects to improve the quality and efficient care of the populations we serve.

DEMONSTRATE RESPECT FOR A DIVERSITY OF EXPERTISE, PERSPECTIVES, INTERESTS, AND VALUES

Ecosystem leaders put their assumptions about each organization or sector to the side. They seek to understand how other stakeholders formed their specific and differing viewpoints and what might make it difficult for those other stakeholders to see the situation as they do. They take time to understand the guiding purpose and mission of each stakeholder organization, how they operate to fulfill that mission, and what metrics are important to them.

Most important, they take the time to ask a lot of questions, and they *actively* listen to the answers. Successful conveners of a collaboration project give each speaker their full attention, and they are good at being psychologically silent. They avoid the tendency to reload—to mentally prepare their own response before they have finished fully listening. Andrew Baskin, MD, vice president and national medical director for quality and clinical policy at Aetna, confirms this vital practice:

> The people leading these efforts must enter the conversation with an openness to try something new and a willingness to utilize the experience of the people sitting around the table. If you value diversity of viewpoints—which at Aetna, we value highly—the conversations come naturally in these new situations.
>
> The ability to accept diverse backgrounds, experiences, knowledge, and perspectives is pivotal. You have to go into these conversations with the recognition that the people you're working with bring as much to the table as you do and listen to their unique input.

Successful alignment needs leaders who encourage each stakeholder to share her background, priorities, and the skills that she brings to the table. They seek to learn what others believe, why they believe it, and what the nature of their goals and requirements might be. Furthermore, because they recognize that each stakeholder can contribute to the work ahead in different ways, they ask each stakeholder to describe what his organization is doing to resolve the specific issue that has been identified and to share other efforts it has been making to improve the health of a specific population.

ENCOURAGE OPEN DIALOGUE AND EXCHANGE OF INTERESTS, IDEAS, EXPERTISE, AND INFORMATION ACROSS STAKEHOLDERS

Ecosystem leaders strive to involve *all* identified stakeholders. They monitor their own airtime, being careful not to monopolize conversations. They focus more on inquiry than on advocacy, and they ask more than they tell. Once they state their views, they stop and ask others for their opinions: "Here's what I am thinking . . . what do you think? What else do you feel should be considered?" They take time to understand the business of others, and when they ask questions, ecosystem leaders pause to listen to what others say and let them talk without interruption.

In chapter 6, David Carmouche of Ochsner observes that a lack of cross-sector understanding can stymie success. He recommends people take the time required for inquiry, explaining that "this could be done just by asking the right types of questions and getting the partner to open up and share how they view the world. Leaders could also ask to spend time within their partners' organizations, which creates opportunities for learning in their environment." David finds that the process of questioning has value beyond the understanding it builds: "The best thing to do to drive alignment is to gain an understanding of your cross-sector partner's business model and ways of thinking."

In pursuing this understanding, successful ecosystem leaders do not draw conclusions too quickly or dismiss others' ideas. They follow up on the answers with more questions, such as, Why is that important to you? or What makes that approach compelling for your organization? Then, as ideas come forward, they look for views that they can agree with and actively recognize and reinforce those perspectives.

Of course, we know that it is never all smooth sailing, and issues and problems will undoubtedly arise. This acknowledgment brings us to our discussion of the next HELM cluster, managing boundaries and obstacles.

KEY TAKEAWAYS

- Aligning stakeholders requires leaders to bring together diverse stakeholders and help them connect around a common purpose, objectives, and areas of focus by:
  - *Seeking connections with others to further a broad purpose.* This approach requires leaders to connect actively with other stakeholders, avoid overstating their position, actively seek contributions from all parties, and encourage the vision to evolve as each stakeholder contributes his ideas.
  - *Taking concrete steps to enable the group to come together effectively and build relationships.* Seek to minimize time conflicts and optimize the available time. Include enough time for people to get to know each other, so you build trust, making it more likely that stakeholders will give each other the benefit of the doubt when (inevitable) tensions arise.
  - *Demonstrating respect for a diversity of expertise, perspectives, interests, and values.* Leaders must put their assumptions about each organization or sectors to the side. They ask questions, actively trying to understand each organization's guiding purpose and mission and the basis for specific and differing viewpoints.
  - *Encouraging open dialogue and exchange of interests, ideas, expertise, and information across stakeholders.* This freedom requires leaders to get everyone involved, to avoid taking over the conversation, and to focus more on inquiry than on advocacy.

REFERENCE

Knowles, M. 2018. "'Sacrifice a Little Profitability to Do the Right Thing for the Patient': Thoughts from Summit Medical Group CEO Dr. Jeffrey Le Benger." *Becker's Hospital Review.* Published February 8. www.beckershospitalreview.com /hospital-management-administration/sacrifice-a-little -profitability-to-do-the-right-thing-for-the-patient-thoughts -from-summit-medical-group-ceo-dr-jeffrey-le-benger.html.

CHAPTER 8

Manage Boundaries and Obstacles

Let me embrace thee, sour adversity, for
wise men say it is the wisest course.

—William Shakespeare, 1591

COLLABORATIVE ECOSYSTEM PROJECTS often face myriad issues that need to be resolved before the initial design plan and implementation plan are agreed to. Matters such as investment, reimbursement, competing organizational cultures and structures, and difficulty in data sharing are typical. The more diverse the stakeholders, the more varied the business models that are operating, and the more likely that there will be points of tension.

As the process moves from exploring goals to developing actions, participants need to discuss and agree on questions of what to do and how to proceed. The potential solutions and the possible approaches to implementation must be formed in the context of the differences in organizational priorities and culture and the political aspects of decision-making and governance. As noted by Barry Ostrowsky of RWJBarnabas Health, again in reference to the citywide effort to address unemployment mentioned in chapter 2:

> One size does not fit all. The goal may be the same among the various organizations within the city, but the specific

success of the program may manifest differently depending on the organization's context. We can look for common ground in standardizing the process, but if you spend too much time trying to figure out a program that fits everybody, you end up with the lowest common denominator and not a lot of progress.

The goals can be agreed upon, but the actual tactical implementation process has to be flexible enough to allow each of the organizations to do it in a way that's more productive for them. For example, publicly traded companies such as PSE&G and Prudential have other oversight with respect to shareholder interest. When they pledge to hire unemployed local people, they need to keep in mind shareholder interest with regard to how it's going to impact the success of the company and what it's going to mean to the value of their stock. These specific organizational contexts need to be taken into consideration when you volunteer for an initiative such as this.

Accurately defining and gaining agreement on roles and responsibilities, resources, information sharing, and decision-making processes are vital, and successful ecosystem leaders recognize these as points of potential tension. The conversations that take place to resolve those issues are the pathway to defining an initial set of actions and agreements. The approach and behavior of the leaders determine how successfully these conversations progress and whether the group can move into action.

As these discussions ensue, the ecosystem leader

- supports constructive conflict,
- focuses on opportunity in the face of disagreement, and
- resolves tension.

SUPPORTS CONSTRUCTIVE CONFLICT

Postponing difficult conversations gives space for misunderstandings and miscommunication between the parties, making challenges even harder to resolve. Health ecosystem leadership model (HELM) leaders must have confidence in their professional gut and in the value of their collective mission and not be afraid to disagree with other stakeholders respectfully, regardless of their role or affiliation. While keeping an open mind, they stick to their guns in the face of pushback and do not lose their composure.

In chapter 6, Bob Hemker of Palomar Health discusses an initiative around a new model of care for behavioral health. He tells us what happened when faced with obstacles to progress:

> First and foremost, I had to understand what this new model was going to entail programmatically. I also had to ensure that all the stakeholders were supportive of the crisis stabilization model. The biggest challenge was engaging and gaining buy-in from the frontline providers, specifically the psychiatrists. They were concerned about what this new model would mean for their practices, and whether their already limited resources would be spread even thinner.
>
> To get them comfortable with this new model and move their "this is how things have always been done" mind-set, we conducted site visits in Alameda [a county in California] so the others could see this different delivery model in action. Gaining buy-in from the stakeholders is really all about making sure their concerns are heard and addressed. Do that and you'll alleviate a lot of tensions.
>
> We also ran into some obstacles in discussions with the county regarding the pay rate. The county has limited

resources, and so their grant dollars and the initial pay rate they offered were not going to be sufficient. Through several positive (and at times, intense) conversations, we were able to agree to an ongoing sustainable care rate.

Thus, we can see that successful ecosystem leaders are prepared to have to deal with people's reactions to change. They respond to objections and any disruptive behavior from others in ways that keep the conversation going, and they never underestimate the effort needed to keep the objectives on track. Even if they feel attacked, they seek to calm the situation by asking clarifying questions or seeking advice from others around the table on what is needed to help move things forward.

Mental rehearsal for tough circumstances is always going to be helpful, as is staying aware of situations that might trigger their own disruptive behaviors. Ecosystem leaders prepare to react constructively. Sometimes, just a little bit of give and take is all that is needed to keep the momentum going and avoid the initiative becoming sidetracked, as evinced by Roland Lyon, president of Kaiser Permanente of Colorado, the state's largest nonprofit healthcare provider:

> I work with my team to determine our priorities—what's most important to us—and then I head off to the discussion table. My top five priorities may be absolutely critical to me, but I have to be ready for a little give-and-take. The other party's top five might not be aligned with mine, but they may also have objectives that are more open to give-and-take as well.
>
> If you concede on one of your top priorities in order for the other party to have one of their priorities met, that goes a long way toward building that relationship of trust. When they see that you are willing to give up something that is important to you for the bigger purpose of finding common ground, that strengthens the relationship.

If you find yourself in such a situation, critical statements that could become an obstacle to progress must be avoided. The alternative is to present the problem in ways that encourage others to engage productively in the discussion and to make it easier to identify common ground. Base what you say on facts, not emotions or opinion; describe specific problems and conditions and their impact on the outcomes that the group is pursuing. Present reasons and concerns before offering solutions and then elicit each party's must-haves, using open questions to seek others' views before sharing your own perspective.

Ecosystem leaders look to highlight areas of agreement as a first step. Once shared interests are defined, the discussion can move to areas of disagreement, which, as we said earlier, should never be ignored. Disagreements provide important information, and the use of open questions helps drive understanding of why those areas are important to the different parties. This understanding continues to help move the discussions to generating solutions. As the conversations continue, leaders support the group in developing a broader view of the possibilities. Thus, new perspectives can emerge.

FOCUSES ON OPPORTUNITY IN THE FACE OF DISAGREEMENT

The structural and cultural differences between organizations can be difficult to reconcile, especially when there is little history of prior interaction. This lack of experience and understanding of others' perspectives, cultures, and drivers often results in potentially false assumptions.

This notion can be applied to each of the different sectors. For example, health plans have their views about clinicians, and clinicians have their opinions about health plans. They both have their views about pharmaceutical companies, and all of them have their beliefs about the capabilities of public health agencies. Frequently, these perceptions are derived from limited exposure and untested assumptions. Differing viewpoints are built from limited interaction with one another, and it takes time to work through those barriers to understand what is important to each party, and to see how others think about the issues at hand.

It also takes a while before the group starts to see results, and the time required to work through tough issues can get in the way of progress and the staying power of all the participants. Resolution is time-consuming and challenging work, and it often conflicts with the primary responsibilities of the people who need to come together to get the work done. Thus, tensions will naturally arise as part of the voyage to innovative solutions, but the essential point is that leaders must not be distracted. Instead, the leader who understands how to work across the ecosystem stays focused on what needs to be achieved.

Josh Ofman of Amgen offers his perspective of how his organization stays focused on mutually beneficial opportunities:

> It's critical for the success of these partnerships to keep the parties' interests aligned on a shared goal as opposed to enhancing one organization or the other. For Amgen, we engage in partnerships where we feel we can make a difference on population health as opposed to focusing only on Amgen products.
>
> With United Healthcare, a major payer in the health industry, our collective interests were well aligned on the patient. When we run into situations where the financial interests are the primary focus or significantly divergent, we choose not to pursue. If it's seen as just a business tactic, these collaborations tend to stall or fall apart.

As you can see, advocates of HELM do not allow immediate concerns to distract them from their purpose and goals. As David Carmouche further suggests, the answer is often to seek some common ground, then leverage that in order to keep the initiative going:

I am the only member of Ochsner's senior management team that comes from a payer background, giving me a unique perspective to anticipate potential obstacles and suggest methods to overcome the roadblocks in a win–win manner. For example, if someone on my team starts speaking from a position that is historical or from a provider-focused angle that I know is in conflict with how the payer views the world, I'll call it out and help them understand the other side's position.

Getting both parties to understand the other's side is very difficult, though. If you can paint your position in a very clear-cut, understandable, and factually based manner, that tends to move people. If you can also figure out what the middle ground looks like, and what each side has to do to get there, that tends to be an effective way to move people who are hesitant. Even the most recalcitrant people tend to take a step forward when they see that the other party is willing to meet halfway. That's the tactic that's been helpful for me.

To ensure that common goals are met, ecosystem leaders focus on the unique value that needs to be delivered, not the activities. They are clear that the only good solution is one that can ultimately be implemented, and ecosystem leaders recognize in these successful solutions the contributions of *all* the parties to the outcome and vision that have been articulated. In order to achieve that state, and keep a focus on the positive, they view conflict as an opportunity.

Healthy debate is seen as a vehicle to better solutions, sometimes even a so-called third way that is different from any party's initial positions. Effective ecosystem leaders put difficult issues on the table, because they know that leaving them unspoken and unresolved can place the overall effort in jeopardy. As the discussion unfolds, they listen to objections and acknowledge the concerns of all the stakeholders, always redirecting the conversation to the common purpose and goals.

RESOLVES TENSION

As common ground is identified and each party has had the opportunity to articulate their must-haves, the leader can begin to define solutions. She must now ask all parties to demonstrate that they are committed to creating solutions that will satisfy the overall interests of the group—it's that put-up-or-shut-up moment.

Thus, the key to resolving tension is to work proactively with all stakeholders to generate a variety of options. Initially leaders should avoid taking a hard-line position and instead set an objective of generating as many alternative approaches as possible. When ecosystem leaders demonstrate a willingness to give up on some of *their* interests to achieve the common goals, they are in a much better position to ask this of others.

To underscore this point, here's Roland Lyon from Kaiser Permanente of Colorado again:

> Working through tension points to align on interests takes quite a bit of discussion and requires that all parties articulate why they want what they are proposing, and not just the "what" itself. You have to dig deeper than the "what" to discover reasons that are aligned. It is only then that parties can work to find a solution that's mutually beneficial. Of course, a degree of give-and-take also exists since we all have our different priorities.
>
> The parties have to be willing to sacrifice a little, which can only occur when there is mutual respect, transparency, authenticity, willingness to listen, and a bit of humility. The last piece of it is just compromise, plain and simple.

As illustrated by Roland's experience, generating discussion is critical to avoiding or relieving tension. While it presents risks, open and direct dialogue is the primary route to sustainable solutions that are equitable for multiple stakeholders, and those risks can be mitigated. Alternatives can be explored initially, avoiding commentary or editing, and this open exploration helps all of the stakeholders see the pros and cons of the various solutions.

As the discussion moves forward, a definition of success emerges that can set the stage for ensuring that tensions do not remain unresolved. In this regard, David Carmouche tells us of a situation in which tensions and conflicting interests among various stakeholders were effectively managed in order to advance collaboration with a vital partner:

> For Ochsner to remain successful, we needed to be able to sell narrow-network products, since these offer cheaper premiums, which appeal to price-sensitive consumers. If we were going to be taking utilization down and if the per-capita reimbursement to Ochsner was going to decrease, then we needed more capita.
>
> The way to grow was to either capture more of the healthcare services within our system or to bring new people into our system who didn't historically get their care here. That required a narrow-network vehicle that has benefits designed to keep people within our system.
>
> The challenge was that most of the business that we were going after was controlled by brokers. Blue Cross had mastered the distribution of their products through great relationships with brokers, but brokers don't like narrow networks because they don't understand them, and they have to deal with a lot of postsale complaints by employees who are no longer able to go to the physician or facility of their choice. Furthermore, their brokerage

fees are the same for selling these products even though they require more work.

For us to collaborate successfully with Blue Cross, we needed to consider how to change the incentives for brokers. It had been very difficult for Blue Cross to think through how to do that because they were very afraid of disrupting their relationship with their brokers. To overcome this, we pulled together a meeting between some of their most influential brokers, Blue Cross's sales and marketing team, and my team at Ochsner, to explain that our imperative was to lower the cost of health insurance, and that the way for Ochsner to do that—and remain viable and successful—was through narrow-network products.

It was really important to open that dialogue with the brokers because it could have potentially been a disruptive move in the marketplace. Much of the feedback we received from the brokers was that, had we not brought everyone together and explained that vision, they probably would have fought us tooth and nail.

But we knew we had to align all the players because everyone comes in with their different priorities for their own organization. By opening up the dialogue and laying everything out on the table in a very transparent way, we were able to come up with a collaborative solution.

We can learn from that story that in moving toward lasting and meaningful solutions to health-related problems, ecosystem leaders look for ways to minimize the negative impact of those solutions on each stakeholder. All stakeholders must be encouraged to work together to ensure that everyone is clear on, and can articulate, the benefits they will realize from the emerging solution.

When discussions become difficult, ecosystem leaders must step back and ask themselves and the group to consider the consequences of not generating a viable solution. Then, as something emerges that both serves the vision and purpose of the group, and that can be embraced by each of the key stakeholders, the focus can move to implementing the first set of actions. This phase is the first critical component of Act and Learn, the final HELM cluster discussed in the next section.

KEY TAKEAWAYS

- Managing boundaries and obstacles requires leaders to engage in conversations that will determine how successfully the group can resolve conflict and move into action by doing the following:
  - *Supporting constructive conflict.* Leaders must present the problem in ways that encourage others to engage productively and to identify common ground, disagree respectfully, keep an open mind, and support the group in developing a broader view of possibilities and new perspectives.
  - *Focusing on opportunity in the face of disagreement.* Leaders should view conflict as opportunity, listen to objections, acknowledge concerns, redirect conversations to the common purpose and goals, and identify solutions that optimize the contributions of all parties.
  - *Resolving tension.* Resolution requires leaders to work proactively with all stakeholders to generate options—and then solutions—that satisfy the overall interests of the group and achieve common goals.
- Ecosystem leaders look for ways to minimize the negative impact of solutions on each stakeholder and ensure that they understand and can articulate the benefits associated with the emerging solution.

CHAPTER 9

Act and Learn

A journey of a thousand miles begins with a single step.

—Lao-Tzu, fourth century BCE

No matter how small, first steps represent incremental progress and help to motivate continued action. Simply identifying the resources needed to begin building new capabilities required for the solution is a demonstrable initial action. With those first steps accomplished, the ecosystem leader can look for more to be adopted, developed, and implemented as consistent with the agreed areas of focus.

As Poonam Alaigh, formerly of the US Department of Veterans Affairs, notes:

> One of the biggest challenges in achieving successful collaboration is the lack of demonstrable progress and not celebrating the small successes. It's the notion that we have to fix perpetuating problems rather than recognizing the small wins along the way. It's the fact that we focus on what is not working rather than look at what is working. It is how we regress to our siloes instead of continuing to work as interdependent teams that value the collective contribution.

Change in healthcare is not just a flip of a switch. It takes time and patience to turn this big ocean liner around. Collaboration becomes stronger when we showcase our improvements and strengths in a tangible way, while simultaneously being transparent about the vulnerabilities and weaknesses in the system that still need improvement.

The team has to appreciate the milestones and successes made along the journey while recognizing that more work needs to be done. Collaborations are successful when teams recognize they can alternate between jogging and sprinting while running a marathon.

Successful health ecosystem leaders initiate actions to advance the vision as a way to learn. As steps unfold, the progress and outcomes of the actions are observed and used to inform next steps. The feedback gathered often leads to the further evolution of the purpose and focus, more discussion of boundary issues, the identification of new obstacles, and the definition of the next set of actions.

During this process, the ecosystem leader demonstrates the principles of the final cluster of the health ecosystem leadership model (HELM), Act and Learn:

- Plan action steps
- Enact concrete steps
- Act despite uncertainty
- Use feedback to adapt plans and advance the vision

PLAN ACTION STEPS

Plans must be transparent to all participants so that there is a shared understanding of the objectives, the actions to achieve those, and the measures that will assess the outcomes. Effective ecosystem leaders take the time to ensure all parties understand what is intended to be accomplished and that all stakeholders are aware of any associated risks.

In defining what needs to be done, leaders break the ecosystem solution into its component parts. They don't expect, or necessarily try to get, the solution totally right at the outset. They understand that the more complex and uncertain the situation, the more important it is to take incremental steps. They understand (and prefer) small steps and quick feedback to long time frames and few data.

For example, Donna Mills of the Central Oregon Health Council (COHC) describes the process used to advance the Regional Health Improvement Plan (RHIP) she discussed in chapter 6:

> The current process includes workgroups aligned with each of the RHIP areas of focus, who collectively decide how they can impact change and improve the health of our communities. Each of these groups, with a COHC facilitator, uses the Lean tool known as *A3* to fully understand gaps, measures, and impact on the current metrics.
>
> Upon completion, they will look at strategic investment opportunities and requests; they may consider several key tactics, such as funding, aligning incentives, contracts, policy, demographic focus, maintenance, and/or aligning efforts. Each workgroup is seeded with $250,000.

Journalist Lola Butcher (2017, 7) presents a case study of the Milwaukee Health Care Partnership's initiative to identify and address community health needs. Joint community health needs assessments helped the health systems zero in on shared priorities, and the article reported on the outcomes:

> [Via] individual analysis, each health system reviews the shared CHNA [community health needs assessment] to help advance its own community health improvement plan. For example, when the most recent CHNA was published

in 2016, Froedtert Health shared the findings with all of its hospitals through its Community Health Improvement advisory committees.

These committees include community members and health system leaders. Members of the committees rated each of the priority areas based on two criteria: Froedtert Hospital's ability, as the region's academic medical center, to address that particular need and the likelihood of achieving measurable outcomes.

That process identified four community health needs to be addressed by Froedtert Health's three-year community health improvement plan:

- Chronic disease management.
- Injury and violence.
- Access to care and navigation.
- Behavioral health.

Action plans were developed for each of the four needs. For example, Froedtert Hospital, in collaboration with the Medical College of Wisconsin, launched a pilot of the Cardiff Violence Prevention Model in conjunction with a suburban police department.

Ecosystem leaders who engage with each other to build an action plan know that multiple, smaller actions expand the opportunity to learn, get things right for the long term, and help to manage risk. The plans they create are designed to test assumptions and ideas as simply and inexpensively as possible, particularly in the early stages. Progress goals and measures are used to inform the direction and next steps more than to measure final success. Here is Tanisha Carino again, further discussing the collaborative work she did with America's Health Insurance Plans while at GSK:

As a group, we came up with three focus areas and were aligned on immediate actions that could be taken to achieve these goals. These areas included:

- What evidence needed to be generated to improve adult immunization?
- What types of data infrastructures should be established to capture the data?
- What kinds of incentives needed to be established and funded to support improvements in adult immunization?

We pulled together our action plans in a white paper to create a road map for solutions that we (as a collective group of interested stakeholders) could advance.

And as Lorie Shoemaker, chief nursing executive of Catholic Health Initiatives, Texas Division, built her plan, she was very aware of the need to learn from what occurred as the actions rolled out: "It's also important to identify the outcome metrics for how we know if we've been successful. We also need to hold each other accountable by drafting a project plan and identifying the responsible party for each step. That way, when we reconvene, we will know what progress we have made and where we need to improve."

ENACT CONCRETE STEPS

Creating a plan that breaks the proposed solutions into components allows the ecosystem leader to implement incrementally. These incremental steps expand the opportunities to learn from what works and what doesn't. By building the plan in this way, the ecosystem leader sets the stage to test the assumptions built into the solution. As the actions unfold, the results of each experiment can be reviewed and the findings used to modify assumptions and adapt future actions.

Even the most results-oriented individuals understand that working on a collaborative initiative requires a learning process. Here's David Carmouche of Ochsner:

> I have had to learn to take a longer-term view. I am not a patient person—I see an opportunity and have a vision for our organization that is so powerful to me that I want to get to it immediately. For me, the leadership lessons have been that you're not going to hit a home run on every complex initiative, and that there is value in just having the discussion itself.
>
> Not reaching the desired solution immediately doesn't equate to failure. Just opening up the dialogue and having the conversation makes the organization better and is part of their growth. For me, it's recognizing it as a learning process that takes time and persistence.

ACT DESPITE UNCERTAINTY

Ecosystem leaders accept that they are often sailing into uncharted waters, and they are prepared to take reasonable risks to keep the initiative moving forward toward a solution. Driven by the potential gain when the risk pays off, they build and articulate a business case for the chances being taken. They realize that inaction and overanalysis constitute risk and that failure can result from doing nothing.

Even if something does not work, it can lead to an alternative that does—that is the essence of the Act and Learn cluster of HELM. Consider this example from Carman Ciervo of Jefferson Health New Jersey, who took action on a potentially beneficial health initiative for his organization's community, even when the outcome of the initiative was unforeseen:

There was one initiative that was dropped on my radar, and it was up to me to determine how to handle it with minimal information for how to approach it. We had decided initially to go with a retail strategy, where we were going to put other primary care offices in the community. That initiative was what I'd call "primary care on steroids" because it was open every day including holidays, but the ROI [return on investment] on that ended up being costly. It didn't work for us because patients didn't necessarily gravitate to a particular venue—they were gravitating to particular areas of the community. We had to regroup and recognize that it was not a worthy investment.

Ecosystem leaders recognize that some risks won't pay off. They work to create an environment where it is OK to fail and learn from mistakes. They are confident navigators, and enter the process knowing that problems can be fixed, plans will be modified, and the vision will likely evolve.

USE FEEDBACK TO ADAPT THE NEXT STEPS AND PLANS TO ADVANCE THE VISION

Leaders need to set expectations early on that adapting the approach and shared vision is an expected part of the process. As the initial plans move forward, they establish checkpoints to measure progress, share promising results, and celebrate wins. Effective leaders look at what can be learned. Using that information, they explore the need to change the plan or approach. After, action reviews are used to generate learning. The group asks, "What were our objectives? What part of the solution worked? Which objectives were not achieved? What positive attributes do we want to retain as we move forward? What should be different the next time?"

Ecosystem leaders use this process to seek out common elements in successes and failures and to integrate learning into their next steps. As Carman Ciervo notes earlier in the chapter, the action strategy of placing primary care offices in retail locations did not result in the intended outcomes, and so the plan was modified based on feedback and learning in order to have a greater impact. "What we learned was that we needed our initiatives to align with our core strategy of understanding our community and providing primary care access points in places where the services are most likely to be utilized. You can't just attach it to a Walmart or some other large chain and expect that people will want to get their healthcare there too. We knew we wanted to provide access points to people in the community, but the ones that bear the most fruit are the ones that are inculcated within the community."

While they are open to making changes to improve the solution, ecosystem leaders focus on the steps that make the most sense. They reexamine all aspects of the plan: "Do we need to define the issue differently? Should we eliminate or recombine some of our solution elements?" They may revisit their initial problem statement and solutions to see if they need to look for some new answers.

Throughout the review, ecosystem leaders stay focused on the ultimate goal and actively demonstrate continued commitment to the overall purpose. The learning process helps advance the vision, identify new stakeholders, and modify the approach and agreements . . . for the next ecosystem initiative.

KEY TAKEAWAYS

- The Act and Learn cluster of HELM requires leaders to take steps toward advancing the shared vision that was created at the outset of the collaboration by doing the following:
  - *Defining plans and taking concrete action.* Leaders must understand that change does not happen overnight and that concrete, tactical action steps with defined

indicators must be planned and enacted to get the ball rolling.

- *Acting despite uncertainty.* Even when the path forward is unclear, collaborative leaders take reasonable steps to keep the plan in motion, knowing that inaction and overanalysis can hinder progress.
- *Using feedback to adapt the next steps and plans to advance the vision.* Even when the collaborative solution does not go as planned, leaders accept that it is an evolving process and correct the course as necessary.

REFERENCE

Butcher, L. 2017. "Case Study: Milwaukee Health Systems Partner to Identify and Address Community Health Needs." *H&HN.* Published October 13. www.hhnmag.com/articles/8628-case -study-milwaukee-health-systems-partner-to-collectively-identify -and-address-community-health-needs.

Grasping the Opportunity for Meaningful Change

*[Creativity is] giving yourself permission
to see things differently.*

—David Robert, 2016

THROUGHOUT OUR BOOK, we have illustrated our theories with practical evidence from real-life situations experienced by our various ecosystem leaders. This approach continues in chapter 10, which presents a detailed case study of a leader who demonstrates the behaviors in our health ecosystem leadership model (HELM) as she builds an ecosystem solution.

Although some elements are fictitious for the purposes of storytelling, much is based on real events, and therefore names have been changed. These events represent the challenges and opportunities that we have encountered, either as health industry executives ourselves or while coaching our clients, in creating and implementing cross-sector ecosystem solutions.

As we have explored, ecosystem collaborations seek to improve the overall health of communities; thus, we believe it is extremely important that initiatives such as the one we describe in this chapter become more visible and grow exponentially. Numerous stakeholders and other parties are involved in this story. To help you identify them all, we offer exhibit 10.1.

Exhibit 10.1: Stakeholders in the Ecosystem Initiative

Sector	Name	Title
Provider	Heather Mitchell	President, Wellington Community Hospital (WCH) (one of six community hospitals in CHS)
Provider	Amy Nicholson	President and CEO, Channel Hospital System (CHS) based in Maryland
Provider	Glen Cross	President, Prenton Community Hospital (one of six community hospitals in CHS)
Provider	Dan Liu	Vice President of Finance, WCH
Provider	Bijan Rezaei	CFO, Channel Hospital System
Provider	Frank Brady	President and CEO, Metro Health System
Executive coach	Samantha Geary	President, Health Ecosystem Coaching and Consulting Group, LLC
Payer	LaTanya Simpson	Vice President of Provider Relations for Integra Health Plans
Community health	Sonia Hernandez	Consumer Advocate for the township of Wellington
Patient with diabetes	Daria Rahal	Wellington resident
Pharmaceutical company	Phillipe Santiago	Vice President of Hospital Contracts for Xacta Pharmaceuticals
Clinicians	Sojin Park	Chief Medical Officer and Chief Population Health Officer for CHS
Retail pharmacy	Raj Patel	Senior Vice President of Strategic Partnerships for VIA Drug Stores
Town council	Michelle O'Grady	Mayor of Wellington
Transportation	Tony DeMarco	Owner, WellGO Drivers

DECEMBER 1: CHS BOARD AND
EXECUTIVE LEADERSHIP RETREAT

Our story begins one morning in the boardroom of Channel Hospital System (CHS), where Heather Mitchell is about to begin a presentation.

Heather Mitchell, president of Wellington Community Hospital (WCH), sat at the head of the oval conference room table, while her boss, Amy Nicholson, CEO of CHS, spoke of the vital importance of the meeting to attendees. As Amy spoke, Heather reviewed her notes for the final time. She wasn't nervous about speaking. However, along with Amy, she simply wanted to make sure that her message and the lessons she had learned got across to the board and her colleagues.

Because her initiative reflected her professional passion for affecting healthcare outcomes, and because she knew what a difference her initiative made, she was excited to explain her journey and the struggles she had faced as well as the successes resulting from her efforts. With all of Amy's board, as well as Heather's peers (the presidents of the other six hospitals that made up CHS) present, this bunch could be tough to convince. However, she had faith that the many improvements she had achieved would present a compelling argument for the value of cross-sector partnerships and would provide motivation for her colleagues to embark on ecosystem collaborations themselves.

Heather thought back to the moment when she had initially approached Amy with her ideas. She was met with some resistance, receiving only a cautious green light. However, as Heather made progress she was able to engage her boss fully. As real breakthroughs were made, Heather had suggested bringing in the other hospitals in CHS. However, Amy told her to wait. The first time her peers heard about what Heather had been doing, Amy wanted them to see a more complete picture, where the results and effort required to execute could not be doubted. Now Heather knew Amy had been right.

After a few minutes' further preamble, Amy asked Heather to deliver her presentation. The first slide on the screen behind her showed:

Live WELLington!
A Health Collaboration
Initiative

"I know everyone recognizes that our system is currently operating in a state of uncertainty," Heather began. "Value-based reimbursement schemes are clearly the direction the industry is headed, yet most hospitals—our own included—are still mainly being paid on a fee-for-service schedule. And, while we know we need to do more in our communities, programs that improve community health aren't reimbursed. In fact, when they work, they cost us revenue.

"Much like you, I felt stuck. Nevertheless, I knew that we needed to find a way to lower cost, create value, and improve outcomes for our patients and the community of Wellington. Today, I hope that after I share the ideas and the approaches I took, you'll be motivated to pursue value-based population health solutions in your communities as you continue to lead your entities within CHS.

"Amy has already confirmed her belief in the importance of what I have to share with you today, and in doing so, she mentioned I've been doing a lot of work recently to manage the total cost of care. While I plan to talk more about that later, I'd like to focus first on the key drivers that affect health, such as obesity, physical inactivity, smoking, stress, and aging.

"As far back as 2002, J. Michael McGinnis, Pamela Williams-Russo, and James R. Knickman reported that while most of the efforts of the healthcare industry focused on healthcare, treatment of sickness contributed a mere 10 percent to the prevention of premature death when compared with the impact of other health determinants, such as environmental exposure, behavioral patterns, and socioeconomic status. This is still the case today.

"That's why when I took on the *total* cost of care, I knew I had to think more broadly than the services that we at WCH provide. We are just one cog in the wheel of cost. If we are to bend the cost curve, we need to consider how other broad drivers contribute to the overall cost of care. As soon as I began to consider things from this *different* perspective, I recognized the existence of many other players, way beyond our usual four walls, who ought to be working with us on effective and sustainable solutions."

Heather paused there to sip some water, and already she could see that one of her peers, Glen Cross, had an "I'm not interested in all this" look on his face. Heather was not surprised because she knew that willingness to truly collaborate with others was not exactly prevalent in the broader health industry. Everybody tended to focus on her own mission, objectives, and metrics. Even when people did try to cooperate, each person's organizational interest was an obstacle to success.

Heather had learned that true collaboration required a different type of mind-set. She had come to understand the importance of acting in ways that allowed trust to be created and new relationships to form. That was so important when things got tense, which they usually did. Yes, some people have natural collaboration skills. Other people—such as Glen—would have to work at it.

Sure, if challenged to ask more questions, really listen to the answers, and recognize what was important to others before stating his own opinion, Glen would say, "Of course, that makes sense. I do that all that time." Yet Heather knew from her own experience that Glen had a hard time keeping quiet and listening to others; when he was quiet he was usually checking his phone for messages.

"While we all like to lead from our comfort zone," continued Heather, trying not to look in Glen's direction, "right now, there was never a greater need to challenge our preconceived notions and think beyond our own operating model. Here in Wellington, we have started to look at the cost of care in a pre- and post-acute environment, seeking to determine who needs to be involved with us to manage both outcomes and cost. It's been causing us to look at things from a much broader perspective, to take in the views of our community, and seek to *truly* understand where the costs come from and where we can make a *real* difference in our community's health.

"For people to live healthier, more productive lives, we need to recognize that no single entity, or, for that matter, no single sector, can or should act alone, but instead many different silos need to contribute. There needs to be a focus on improving community health, asking such questions as, Is this right for the patient? How do we change the way healthcare is delivered? How can we promote wellness? What is our role in supporting healthy populations?

"These are big, big things to resolve, so let me take you back to where it all started . . ."

JANUARY 2 (11 MONTHS PRIOR TO THE CHS BOARD AND EXECUTIVE LEADERSHIP RETREAT)

With a sigh, Heather put aside the latest finance report and buzzed her administrative assistant to ask her to get Dan Liu, her vice president (VP) of finance, on her calendar. Numbers were his focus, and he always seemed to come at them from a different vantage point from Heather's. The issues lay in the fact that no matter what she tried, she just couldn't keep on doing more for less, which was what Dan—and the company's chief financial officer, Bijan Rezaei—were always pushing for. Now, as the reimbursement approaches were moving more toward value, the finance guys were concerned that income would fall dramatically.

Heather had always looked for opportunities to make improvements, and in continuing to do so, she was excited about the opportunity to use some of the data now available through electronic health records to improve care processes. However, she was beginning to recognize that even more would be possible if she began to expand her attentions outside the four walls of her hospital.

There was no way she could succeed when continually being asked to provide more value and better service with diminishing revenue. It was getting harder and harder to stay focused on the reason she had entered this profession—to contribute to the health of the community. The changing payment methods were giving her an opportunity to reconnect with those motives; things such as the Triple Aim went far beyond what her reimbursement contracts recognized.

The report ignored for now, she turned on her monitor and saw a sea of unread emails—she had received more than 50 in the 40 minutes she'd been gone for her last meeting. She was about to ignore them when one subject line caught her eye. It was an invitation to a conference on health ecosystems. She'd been doing some reading recently about initiatives that involved collaborations among organizations from different sectors of the health industry. Despite the fact that such ideas might have merit, she had a very busy hospital to run and didn't feel as though she had the time to attend the conference.

She clicked on the link to the conference site and half-heartedly scanned the brochure. Shaking her head and thinking, "I don't have time for this," she was about to leave the site when she spotted that the keynote address was to be given by one of the most well-respected health system executives in the country, Frank Brady. She had met Frank in New York, and she knew that his health system, consistently rated as top in the nation, was three times the size of hers. The subject of his speech was creating value through cross-sector collaboration. She read the overview of his session and then asked her secretary about her calendar.

FEBRUARY 1: THE HEALTH ECOSYSTEM LEADERSHIP CONFERENCE

Four weeks later, equipped with the obligatory name badge and conference folder, she headed into the hotel's main auditorium. As she sat down, she once more hoped all this would be worthwhile. Within 30 minutes, Heather was scribbling furiously. By lunchtime, she was grateful for her decision to attend that conference.

Over lunch, she managed to catch up with Frank and reviewed the key takeaways of his presentation. She noted the critical points of his address, including the idea that better care, higher quality, and lower costs were possible when you take a collaborative approach.

"You're right," he said. "When you seek to integrate, it's important that you consider your own organization's capacity, and what other key players are doing in the community, from the broadest perspective possible."

"That's fair enough," replied Heather. "So, when organizations commit to community health goals, they need to take a systems approach to achieving the goal—one that considers the various stakeholders that can contribute."

"Exactly!" agreed Frank. "Leaders like us have to sell our vision to our own teams and engage our staff, especially those on the front lines, and also be champions of change outside our own organizations. Much of what leaders must do, in a world that requires cross-sector collaboration, is to rally the troops around a new way of doing work, and that takes constant messaging on the significance of any new initiative and the contribution each party can make to improving health."

As the conversation ensued, Heather became more and more enthusiastic and, as hindsight always does, could not believe why she had not thought of this before. The answers lay in working across her ecosystem, and she knew already from Frank's presentation that her leadership skills—and those of her team—were going to have to change.

DECEMBER 1: BACK AT THE CHS BOARD AND EXECUTIVE LEADERSHIP RETREAT

Heather changed the slide in her presentation. As she did so, she cast a quick glance in Glen's direction. She could see that he had been taking some serious notes on his yellow legal pad, so perhaps he was paying attention? She hoped he'd continue to listen as she discussed her next point. Her slide now simply stated:

**DEFINING
THE PROBLEM**

She began, "When you start to consider an issue with an ecosystem mind-set, the process of defining the problem is vitally important to ensuring that the right people are working on solving the problem with a sustainable solution. For the health issues we tackle, whether it's too many unnecessary emergency department readmissions or poor outcomes, it's important to take as broad a perspective as possible and consider who and what contributes to the problem to ensure you are solving the underlying root causes. It is vital you do this because, and I can't stress this enough, it's virtually impossible to address the health issues that affect our communities alone.

"So, let's now look at the initial steps I took when I got back from the conference. The timing was good because I needed to carry out my annual community needs assessment, which again identified diabetes as a primary health concern of the communities Wellington serves. This illness became the driver for the first work we did with the collaboration team we established.

"We've always taken our annual community needs assessments seriously, but any resulting strategic actions have mostly been focused on what we can control within the hospital. To really influence outcomes of any disease, we need to focus on collaboration—and I'll say it again—outside our own four walls.

"To address this pressing need on a broader basis, we began allocating resources to ensure the right people on my team had shared responsibilities for population health. But where did we start? As suggested, the assessment indicated that our number one community health issue is diabetes. This disease also happens to carry one of the highest total costs of care on our hospital's balance sheet.

"In the past, I've tried all the different, more traditional approaches to improving diabetes and its cost of care. However, the conference inspired me to think differently. Now I knew that if we really wanted to tackle diabetes, make some substantial improvements in both the incidence and prevalence rates, reduce the high cost for routine care, and avoid more admissions resulting from poor disease management, we would need to think and act very differently. Not only did we have an incentive to do this work to reduce the cost to our system, but, more important, it was the right thing to do for the health of the community.

"In addition to thinking about the hospital's role in treating the acute condition, I knew we needed to think much more broadly, to include other elements that influence the long-term health of those with diabetes. For example, we have to start paying attention to what occurs outside our hospital that contributes to readmissions. It's one thing to know the key drivers for maintaining the health of patients with diabetes—we also need to understand what gets in the way in order to create relevant solutions.

"The people I spoke to at the conference recommended that I put together a group of people who represented other sectors, both inside and outside our industry; the community; and other entities that contribute to the health of our patients with diabetes or contribute to their wellness. This is the health ecosystem, and, working together, we can collectively uncover the key issues affecting health and wellness for this disease state. I started with a small group knowing that the team's composition would likely change as we learned more.

"I knew I needed to stay mindful and open to redefining the problem by inviting diverse opinions. Ecosystem collaborative solutions require that you get the right people in the room, and in the process of doing so, you may actually shift the focus of the problem. For example, with our focus on reducing the total cost of care for diabetes, we learned a key issue was medication adherence. Now we knew we needed to understand why this occurred and then create ways to alleviate the roadblocks and make it easier for our patients to stick to their drug treatment plan. This exploration led to further conversations around drug costs, insurance coverage, family makeup, support systems, and a host of other social determinants that influence this disease. More on that later. The point here is that by encouraging dialogue and deepening the conversation around cause and effect, the problem is likely to be refocused."

MARCH 1: HEATHER'S MEETING WITH DAN, VICE PRESIDENT OF FINANCE FOR WCH

The other key person Heather spoke to at the conference who would play a big part in her ecosystem endeavors was Samantha Geary, president of a health industry leadership coaching and consulting firm. Heather heard Samantha speak at the conference in a session titled "How to Engage Others Through Ecosystem Leadership." While the model was simple and clear, it required focused energy to develop the leadership skills Samantha discussed, and Heather was intrigued.

Following the conference, Heather recognized that it was going to be a big adjustment for her to begin to demonstrate the health ecosystem leadership behaviors, so she engaged Samantha as her coach. Heather was soon making good progress. Samantha challenged her assumptions and helped her develop some strategies for finding common ground and build new relationships. Samantha helped her plan for her first postconference meeting with Dan Liu.

Before she went to the conference, any conversation Heather had had with Dan was always negative. She couldn't recall a time when Dan wasn't stressing the importance of cost cutting and budget reductions. While that had been the standard line for everyone in her position since the early 2000s, Heather now recognized that for lasting change that could both decrease long-term costs and enhance the health of the community, they really needed to focus time, energy, and resources on keeping patients out of the hospital. They needed to create tools for individuals at risk of developing diabetes to remain healthy.

While Heather was the final decision maker, she needed Dan to understand her approach. Although she knew it would not be an easy task, her challenge was to get him to see that a short-term focus on cost cutting wouldn't be sustainable. She needed his commitment to a different way of approaching the problem—one that would involve collaborating with others outside her hospital with shared benefits and risks.

"This year was tough, and with the forecast for reimbursements continuing to shrink, we have to ask you to cut costs," was Dan's usual speech, and Heather planned to engage him in a dialogue on her strategy—her first attempt at following Samantha's advice. She was determined to have a different conversation, and she called him into her office. After she gave him some basics on the idea of the ecosystem and improving overall health, she began.

"I know you are concerned about our rate of reimbursement continuing to decline, and so am I. I want to continue our efforts to remove waste from the system and to look for ways to be sure we are consistently using the most effective treatments, and I also think there are some other things we need to begin to do if we are going to truly make sustainable progress. For example, I really want to tackle diabetes like we never have before."

"That sounds great," replied Dan. "Chronic conditions like diabetes really drive a lot of costs for us."

Heather took a deep breath and kept going.

"Exactly, and we know that our patients with diabetes are frequent users of our emergency room, which is the most expensive place for care."

"That's definitely true," said Dan.

"We often find that the people who come to the emergency department have not been taking their medications on a consistent basis. While I know we can't control whether people use their meds appropriately, if we don't address the issue, then I'm going to have more people showing up in my emergency department, and that's going to drive my costs up."

Dan nodded his head in agreement. Had she caught his interest? This was her moment of truth.

"So, I need to have the resources and the time to go out and connect with the right people in our community so we can address that problem. We *have* to invest some resources to get that going."

"But Heather—" he began, and she held her hand to interrupt him. However, her tone was more conciliatory. "As my finance partner, you need to have a stake in this. To get the best out of our system, we need to apply some effort to affecting social determinants. And if we take this need seriously, somewhere along the line, the hospital will likely get into a conversation with other key stakeholders, such as our primary payers and pharmaceutical suppliers."

"Oh, come on!" interjected Dan. "That means we might develop something that saves the payer money—that doesn't help us!"

"Well, perhaps," Heather acknowledged, "and that's where I need your help to negotiate new relationships and create new contracts with stakeholders, so we can work on this problem together and share in the risk and rewards. We are all in the business of health, and it's important to try and get aligned on that common objective. To really do something about diabetes and many of the other conditions that we treat, we have to focus on population health.

"Going forward, successful hospitals will continue to seek ways to deliver services for less while they reduce costs by keeping people *out* of the hospital. I want to talk to the whole team tomorrow, but I wanted to have this conversation with you first because I need your support and expertise. I really want us to try this, and I want to ask the team to think about how we could do a better job of going out and getting other stakeholders involved in this process. I'm talking about stakeholders that we may not have even thought of yet. What do you think they'll say? Will you be with them, Dan?"

"Yeah, yeah. I guess it makes sense. I'm not sure how it will all play out, so I guess we will step into it and see what we can do to move it forward."

MARCH 2: WCH SENIOR
LEADERSHIP TEAM MEETING

That was enough for Heather, and the following day she briefed her senior leadership team with Dan by her side. Some seemed supportive from the start, but she did get some pushback. It was time to turn to the specific words she'd planned before the meeting. She looked at the faces of her direct reports around the room and began.

"With value-based payments on the horizon, we have to step up to become a more integrative, collaborative partner in promoting health and wellness for our community. I'd like our hospital, WCH, to lead this approach for CHS. I want us to be the beacon for the system that shows others the way; I want to demonstrate beyond doubt that we really eat, sleep, and breathe making a difference for our community.

"CHS is undergoing a period of dynamic change, in which issues of affordability, cost, and value are rising to the forefront. As Dan will confirm, the system is increasingly financially strained, and the main culprit is the rising cost of disease and the aging population. The solution to those problems needs to be focused on multiple sectors. We need to identify all players that have a role in the health of the communities we serve and create innovative and collaborative partnerships with those players so that we're not seen simply as a supplier."

As evinced by the nodding heads around the table, Heather thought her statement certainly seemed to do the trick.

MAY 1: FIRST MEETING TO CREATE THE
ECOSYSTEM COLLABORATION

Heather's next step was to do what she had suggested in her meeting with Dan. She reached out to one of their primary commercial and Medicare payers: Integra Health Plans, which covered the majority of the hospital's diabetic patients. While she wanted to explore the idea of a collaborative partnership, first she wanted to get her hands on the insurance company's data to validate the findings from WCH's annual community needs assessment.

Engaging Integra would allow Heather to practice some more of what she had learned during her sessions with Samantha. Her coach had been keen to show Heather that building alignment and trust between diverse stakeholders, such as Integra, would require her to find the common ground. So Heather decided to invite some of Integra's team to talk to her staff to allow both groups to share their unique perspectives on caring for diabetic patients, as well as on trends in total cost of care for their hospital.

Thinking back to her conversations with Samantha, Heather knew that, given her growing enthusiasm for this work, she needed to take her time and not try to jump into convincing the other party that collaboration was the right thing to do. Despite knowing it might not be easy, she really wanted to make her effort a success. She was going to need to work hard on aligning her interests and those of the other stakeholders so they would be willing to approach the process with her.

She also knew she needed to take the time to learn about the issues from their perspectives, what their concerns might be, and how they could be addressed. Frank Brady had told her a variation on Samantha's advice: "Don't walk into the room with a solution. You walk into a room with a purpose, a set of objectives. If you walk in and try to push a solution before you fully get everybody's objectives on the table, you are not going to get there. People look at problems from different angles, and until you are completely aware of all those varying perspectives, you won't be able to see the complete picture."

He continued, "There's an ancient Indian parable about some blind men and an elephant and it's very relevant here. A group of blind men, who have never come across an elephant before, learn and conceptualize what the elephant is like by touching it. Each blind man feels a different part of the elephant's body, but only one part. They then describe the elephant based on their experiences and are in complete disagreement with one another.

"It is only when they stop arguing, start listening, and collaborate that they 'see' the full elephant. The story demonstrates that we have a tendency to project partial experiences as whole truths. The answer to solving complex problems is to talk to people who see the problem differently through their unique experiences."

As Heather approached her meeting with the representatives from Integra, she knew that she had to keep all of this in mind. She needed to manage her own drive to get to a real solution that would address the total cost of care while improving the health and wellness of her patients with diabetes.

Her objective was to get each stakeholder to talk about his assumptions, following up to understand what those assumptions were based on, and use the conversation as a way to get people to open up. It was going to take some effort to practice this different approach, and she thought back to her coaching from Samantha.

"So what if some of those assumptions changed?" Samantha had said. "What if some of the assumptions were based on the past as opposed to the future? Try to encourage the conversation in that way and examine those assumptions to see if they are as relevant going forward as they were previously. Since we've been working together, I've been challenging you on your own assumptions. You now need to do that with your internal and external stakeholders."

Heather had been doing a lot of soul searching, which had helped her with what Samantha had termed *inquiry before advocacy*. You don't know where a conversation is going to go, so you put forth some ideas and try to get a sense of that individual's perspective. The technique had worked with her internal team, and now her next focus had to be on figuring out what was really important to each external stakeholder.

"Just ask *why* five times," Samantha had added. "You ask somebody something and when he replies, you ask why he thinks that, and keep on going until you get to the root of whatever it is you're seeking."

DECEMBER 1: BACK AT THE CHS BOARD AND EXECUTIVE LEADERSHIP RETREAT

After Heather finished reviewing the results from the community needs assessment, she explained to her increasingly interested audience that she was able to corroborate the assessment findings with data that LaTanya Simpson, vice president of provider relations at Integra Health Plans, had agreed to share.

Although it had not been easy at first to get LaTanya to commit, after several meetings of exploring concerns, finding a common interest in helping to keep diabetic patients healthy, and agreeing on some rules of the road, the insurance executive was on board. LaTanya's data helped them identify the most at-risk patients, and that had led to the first of several meetings with a much broader group. Heather pulled up her new slide (exhibit 10.2).

"What we have here are all the various stakeholders that finally came together to take part in our ecosystem collaborative. As you can see, it's very broad, and getting such a diverse group to work together was not easy, but the efforts paid off. The value proposition for being involved was different for all the stakeholders because each one had her own particular interests, and many had risks or downsides to be considered in regard to their varying business metrics.

"However, they all work for organizations that have a shared mission of enhancing health, which was a good rallying point, and they all have different things to offer toward that mission. Collectively, we understood that the whole group had the potential to have a much greater impact on the mission than if any one stakeholder tackled the problem alone.

"This broad view of the drivers and stakeholders of the total cost of care of diabetes developed over time. We didn't start too

Exhibit 10.2: Aligning Stakeholders Around the Patient

Live WELLington! Stakeholders

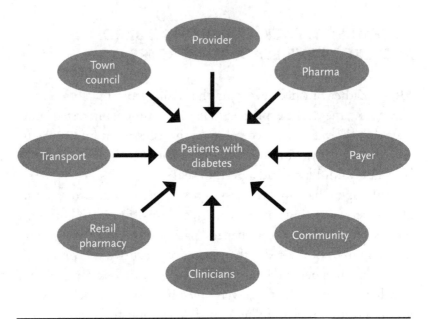

big, but as the conversations progressed, it became sensible to engage some new people. As part of convincing LaTanya Simpson from Integra to join me, I had her meet with Sonia Hernandez, from our Wellington Community Health Department, and Daria Rahal, a patient with diabetes who was frequently admitted to our hospital.

"I provided them with some background and then encouraged Sonia to talk about what efforts the community was leading for diabetic patients, and asked Daria to explain some of the issues she faced and the support she needed. The conversation was enlightening for all of us, especially LaTanya. Now I knew that if we banded together around the patient—as the graphic on this slide suggests—we could really make a difference.

"As that early group converged, it became clear that we needed input and partnership with others, and we decided to broaden the team to include more perspectives. This stage in the collaboration process is all about identifying and aligning stakeholders.

"As you bring more folks together, you continue sharing ideas and perspectives and begin to seek a shared, broader purpose. Sure, it takes time to build relationships; however, there's much value in understanding diverse views as you investigate a solution. Increasingly, I saw my role not as the leader of the effort; rather, I was the convener. While this perspective may be new to your leadership repertoire, my fellow presidents, it is our role as health ecosystem leaders to encourage dialogue and seek other stakeholders' perspectives."

MAY 15: ADDING ANOTHER COLLABORATOR TO THE ECOSYSTEM

In getting others involved, one of the biggest barriers Heather needed to overcome was balancing short-term needs with long-term benefits. For example, there were going to be arguments over who would receive what portion of the pie. Clinicians were reimbursed by payers, as was her hospital. If she was willing to give a bit—and LaTanya was too—then she needed to get the clinicians on board. She had to make the case that a short-term sacrifice would result in a longer-term gain.

"And then the question is, Who benefits?" Frank Brady said when Heather called him one day. "That's where the tension can start. Does the hospital benefit? Does the doctor benefit? Does the payer benefit? What it comes down to is stressing the point that if we keep trying to slice the pie into smaller and smaller pieces and focus only on protecting our own fiefdom, we're all likely to fail. However, if we recognize that these problems have multiple facets to them and that we all can play a role in correcting them, we can somehow redefine the care and wellness model and create a better future for all."

Heather knew that clinician involvement was critical. However, before she tackled that, she opted to approach one of her largest insulin suppliers, Xacta Pharmaceuticals, and got in touch with Phillipe Santiago, vice president of hospital contracts. Knowing that the cost of insulin is a large component of the total cost of care, she wanted Xacta to offer a discount. He agreed to meet, and as Heather approached their first discussion, she remembered that both Frank and Samantha had encouraged her not to drive to a solution too quickly.

She had been advised to give Phillipe an opportunity to express his viewpoint so that she could understand Xacta's perspective on the total cost of care, what his company could be supportive of, what potential obstacles might be, and what Xacta was willing to give on. Based on her progress with LaTanya, she now knew that this approach had a better chance of creating ownership and account-ability, resulting in concrete actions from the very stakeholders who designed them.

Although she wasn't sure how easy it was going to be to get Phillipe on board, it turned out that he was keen to join because he seemed to like the idea of being an innovator. However, he had a strong personality, and Heather now wondered whether she'd be needing Samantha's coaching to keep him on track.

DECEMBER 1: BACK AT THE CHS BOARD AND EXECUTIVE LEADERSHIP RETREAT

"To build shared understanding of the total cost of diabetes care, I invited LaTanya Simpson to join me in the first session with Phillipe. This allowed the three of us to focus on getting our mutual agreement on what we saw as population health, as well as our solo and collective roles in driving improvement, as those who represented the core healthcare sectors affecting the treatment and cost of diabetes care. Here is the slide that got us talking (exhibit 10.3).

"The message is that a true focus on population health will require competing management teams and boards to come together under the shared goal of improving population health. This 'perfect world'

Exhibit 10.3: Partnering to Improve Population Health

IMPROVING POPULATION HEALTH
Partnering for Greater Value

Providers . . .
- Measure outcomes
- Manage variation
- Pass on lower delivery costs
- Innovate

Payers . . .
- Align payment with value
- Reward high-value care with volume
- Continually seek transparency and simplicity

Pharmaceuticals . . .
- Define product value in the context of the care experience
- Establish responsible pricing
- Make value-based commitments
- Adhere to protocol

Source: Courtesy David Carmouche.

scenario illustrates the power of the critical players coming together to transform individual objectives into a collective goal of improved population health. Each player brings his unique strengths to the shared goal and offers relevant best practices to drive the greatest value from our collective efforts.

"With the scene set, I discussed an initiative related to diabetes that brought a major pharma and payer together, and that was a real catalyst for promoting enthusiasm. Briefly, as part of one contract, the drug company assumed some financial risk for its type 2 diabetes medications. If the payer's members with type 2 diabetes taking those drugs didn't meet certain goals, the pharma would pay a rebate to the payer. The other agreement involved a new payer program that used predictive analytics to identify about 500 at-risk patients diagnosed with diabetes. The data were used to create care maps designed to give these patients social support through phone calls and in-person visits from the payer's nurse coordinators.

"In these scenarios, the patient benefits when different parties come together around the shared goal of improving outcomes and controlling costs. The pharmaceutical company assumes some of the risks with the payer. Just getting the parties around the table is a great way to be transparent and diffuse any conflicts of interest."

JUNE 1: ECOSYSTEM COLLABORATIVE TEAM MEETING

At that first meeting Heather held with Phillipe and LaTanya, they suggested sharing savings between her hospital and the physicians if they could report successes in diabetes outcomes based on adherence to medication. It was now time for Heather to bring the doctors to the table as well.

In addition to being the hospital's chief medical officer, Sojin Park also bore the title of chief population health officer and was already a strong advocate for disease prevention efforts in the community. She was very excited to hear about all the efforts Heather had made already. The question now was whether Sojin would be able to enlist the support of her fellow clinicians to agree to join in with whatever future efforts might be on the table—and to help finance them. They both knew that would take time and effort.

At this collaborative meeting, Heather invited additional stakeholders to the table. In addition to Sojin, Phillipe, and LaTanya, Heather invited Sonia Hernandez, who was known to fight hard for the rights of the people in her community. However, she seemed a little in awe of being with all three senior executives for the first time. Using some of what she had learned from Samantha, Heather worked hard to make Sonia feel equal, using encouraging dialogue to draw her in.

This is my view of what can get in the way of people taking their meds as prescribed. What do you think, Sonia? What factors do you see from your vantage point? were typical questions. These seemed to ease Sonia's concerns, and she became an active participant, adding her input to the conversation.

By the end of the meeting, several ideas were beginning to emerge, and, as people packed up their things before departing, a number of enthusiastic conversations were already taking place between seemingly diverse parties. However, Heather had some concerns about Phillipe. While he was certainly in the right role in his company to be on the ecosystem team, he was too quick to jump to solutions when Heather knew that there was still much to be explored. She invited him to dinner, where she shared her observations, and he agreed to be more aware and try to hold back at the next meeting.

JULY 1: ECOSYSTEM COLLABORATIVE MEETING

As they began the next ecosystem meeting, Heather recapped where they were and set out the objectives for the day. Heather stressed the need for everyone to participate in defining the next steps. As the meeting carried on, Phillipe was better at not jumping in and looking for the endgame; however, he now came across as dismissive of the role of social determinants. This attitude quite naturally upset Sonia, and she again became very quiet after he said they should not overcomplicate things and suggested that "these folks just need to be told more clearly that it's critical they take their meds."

Heather proposed a coffee break and took Phillipe to one side. She asked him if he had noticed Sonia's behavior. He had not. "Well if you look at her body language, you can see she's not happy, and she's gone quiet again. What do you think could be going on with her? If you were in her shoes and listening, how would you be hearing the conversation?"

Phillipe paused for a minute. "Well, I think I would be happy that we are all talking but a bit unsure about how I fit in."

"Hmm," said Heather, "Say more."

"Well, we are talking about ways to reduce emergency department admissions for patients with diabetes and a lot of the conversation is around medication compliance."

"That's true," said Heather. "How do you think we could bring her in? Do you see a role for public health?"

Phillipe thought a moment, "Well, maybe we should ask her that?" Heather smiled and said, "Great idea. Perhaps you could do that?" At the end of the meeting, everyone signed off on the next steps, which included Phillipe visiting Sonia at the Community Health Department to see the challenges they faced.

AUGUST–NOVEMBER: ECOSYSTEM COLLABORATIVE TEAM MEETINGS

While the meetings with the broader group continued, work also went on behind the scenes with regard to the clinicians. Heather and Sojin spoke to WCH's chief of endocrinology and asked him for the names of the most influential physicians and allied health professionals in diabetic care. The two women then met with the top three specialists, who recommended another three people, and so on, allowing Heather and Sojin to build support and increase their knowledge of the issues they were tackling through their collaboration. That new outlook set up Sojin to engage and align the physicians in designing programs that focused on the social determinants affecting their diabetic patients, such as access to healthy food and discounts on medications.

Heather's collaboration group now began to follow the agreed-on actions and next steps, and she talked to her internal team again about what it was going to do in the hospital. The staff plan included focused energy on identifying high-risk patients and implementing community outreach programs.

Work began with enthusiasm. Heather wasn't surprised, however, that what they initially tried didn't produce all that they hoped for—she'd expected that some of it would work and some of it would fall short. She was prepared to move forward and learn from what had occurred. When she saw that some of the ecosystem collaboration team members were a little despondent and in danger of abandoning the effort, she sought to rally them again, once more looking at their faces to ensure she had their full attention before she spoke.

"With our ecosystem collaboration group, I am committed to working with all of you to create an implementation plan that includes some metrics we can track that would allow us to test the new ideas as we move forward. Although we may run into some roadblocks and have to regroup, our role as leaders is to act and learn and be willing to take some risk, recognizing that not everything we try will work.

"We are all going to learn as much from what doesn't go well as what does. It can all be continuously modified until we know we are maximizing benefit, and it's vital that we don't lose momentum. We have to be bold and take action, measure the results, and learn from our successes as much as from our failures."

That's what Heather pursued, and while there were some initial successes with projects that were collectively started, some aspects did not work effectively as new learning came to light. Early on, the collaboration group considered the root cause of high readmissions to be failures of medication adherence. With further analysis, it discovered that what got in the way of people taking their medication as prescribed was cost. That's when she knew she needed to leverage her relationship with Phillipe to help lower the cost of treatment.

Despite some early reductions achieved via the discount from Phillipe, Heather was still getting a high number of readmissions. Alongside Sonia, she interviewed a number of these patients and found there was a lack of education related to healthy diet and exercise. Now the group looked to Sonia and the Community Health Department for assistance in providing better education and information on healthy, low-glycemic recipes.

In addition, they clearly recognized that ultimately the best way to reduce cost was to prevent diabetes. The group focused on keeping people well through targeted education about diabetes and what causes it as they sought to prevent incidence rates from rising in the community. To this end, the members continued their efforts and explored how to offer discounts to the community for healthy food choices.

As these plans were being put in place, the team realized that some of Wellington's citizens lived in areas without access to healthy food. They then recommended bringing in the mayor and a local cab company. Based on suggestions from Frank, Heather also invited Raj Patel from VIA Drug Stores, the biggest local retail pharmacy.

Heather continued to push to get plans into place and addressed any issues or matters of fine-tuning with the appropriate stakeholders, determining the best ideas and actions on which they could move forward. Heather was seeing real breakthroughs and finally reached the point at which she and Amy agreed that she should explain the results to the other presidents and CHS's board.

DECEMBER 1: BACK AT THE CHS BOARD AND EXECUTIVE LEADERSHIP RETREAT

It was time to share the details of HELM, which she followed under Samantha and Frank's guidance. With the help of a slide, she explained its four components (exhibit 10.4).

"I've already alluded to future envisioning, stakeholder alignment, and the removal of any blockages to progress. Then I spoke about acting, and learning, and acting again to fine-tune our endeavors, and the more I got into it I began to internalize how that framework would work for myself.

"So, here we have a circle, perhaps a wheel if you will, and as the convener, initially I saw myself as the central hub—much as the patients were in the previous slide—with each of the stakeholders I'd brought together as spokes of the wheel. If none of the parts of the wheel talk to each other, then we have a problem, so I had to align them.

Exhibit 10.4: Health Ecosystem Leadership Model (HELM)

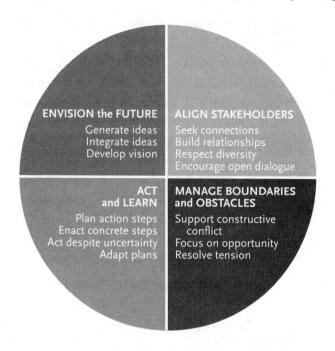

"In the first meeting, when I was beginning to explain where we were and how I wanted us to work together and so on, I had an aha moment—*I* am not the center at all. The hub of all our activity, what's really in the center, is the patients and the needs of the community. I was just another stakeholder, and if we could all align, then we could all be working collectively toward the common goal of creating better health. That message became very powerful in the drive for a singular focus, and it is the idea behind that previous slide of all the stakeholders, which I will return to now."

Heather paused to rearrange her notes before she continued with her presentation, now with her "circle of stakeholders" slide put back on the screen. "Over the course of a four-month period, we held several full-day retreats with the group and some other shorter ad hoc meetings. It was fun and rewarding, and also frustrating and challenging."

"Now that brings me finally to what we all eventually agreed on," Heather said as she gestured to the papers on their table. "I've prepared full information packets for you with my slides from today and a summary of my presentation. It also contains all the details regarding the ecosystem collaborative's outcomes, as well as what we had to address and overcome, which I will discuss now.

"Getting to this point took a lot of hard work and determination, as well as some trial and error along the way. However, I'm sure you will agree that it clearly demonstrates the power of ecosystem collaborations and how much they can benefit each stakeholder as well as, of course, improving the health of our communities. I'll walk you through what each stakeholder contributed, beginning with LaTanya and Integra Health Plans.

"As mentioned, Integra's Medicare plan and its private insurance plans cover the majority of our hospital's diabetic patients. Through our work together, Integra agreed to focus on improving the health and wellness of its members by promoting and funding discounts to local gyms and health food stores for its diabetic members. Naturally, these programs will cost money, but, as LaTanya herself pointed out, it's far cheaper to pay for discounted gym memberships and discounts to healthy food stores than to be paying for costly inpatient visits. Further, they agreed that if these programs result in cost savings, they will offer discounts on premiums to patients for following through on diabetic plans.

"LaTanya also, of course, gets bragging rights that Integra created a diabetic wellness program and the mayor, Michelle O'Grady, is featuring it in a big way in the town newspaper and on the town's website for promotion in the community. This attention all adds up to great press for Integra as it competes for additional commercial and Medicare contracts.

"As suggested, with Phillipe Santiago and Xacta, we have negotiated a significant reduction in the cost of insulin treatments for WCH. In exchange for the discount, we now have an exclusive contract with Xacta as our sole insulin provider. In fact, the price we've managed to negotiate is so good that CHS is now entering negotiations for exclusive contracts for our other hospitals, and each of you, my fellow presidents, will reap this reward."

Here Heather looked around the room, and none of her peers seemed to be annoyed by Heather's independence. Even Glen looked happy now.

"VIA Drug Stores, our retail pharmacy, agreed to support the work of our community physicians. Now all six of the local pharmacies in Wellington have a walk-in clinic, and once per week one of our hospital's nurse practitioners is on-site to offer diabetic screenings and education. If they identify a person as prediabetic, that person gets referred to a hospital-affiliated physician for preventative treatment. The pharmacy has agreed to fund the nurse practitioner's salaries in return for the added value that they provide to customers. VIA is already seeing increased foot traffic and a subsequent boost in revenue.

"Next we come to our clinicians. We were very fortunate to have Sojin on our team. As you are aware, Amy very much wants you to develop your own collaborations, and Sojin has kindly agreed to help you when you brief your own medical staffs. What we determined would help us most was for our clinicians to begin asking their patients questions regarding the social determinants that are influencing their disease. They agreed to work with our collaborative ecosystem team to create an assessment that includes questions about social issues, where the results lead to some form of action.

"Now, of course, we were met with complaints from our physicians about the extra time and frustration of 'yet another form to complete.' To thwart these concerns, Dan has agreed to provide a small monetary incentive to the physicians for each assessment completed. And then there's the other benefit that Frank Brady suggested would occur. As we know, physicians who connected with their patients on issues affecting their health receive higher patient engagement scores and, as incentives are tied to their Hospital

Consumer Assessment of Healthcare Providers and Systems scores, higher income as well.

"The results of the assessments, tied together with the analytics from Integra and our own electronic health record, helps to identify which patients are most critical in terms of social determinants. For example, patients flagged for poor eating habits resulting from food insecurity are supplied with food vouchers eligible for use at local healthy food markets. For this innovation, we enlisted the help of our mayor to entice our local stores to participate.

"As another example, patients flagged for missed appointments are supplied with a voucher for transportation, another key social determinant. For this solution, we negotiated with Tony DeMarco, the owner of Wellington's premier transportation service, WellGO. He is now offering excellent discounted rates for our diabetic patients, which can be used to go to and from doctor's appointments, health food stores, and the gym. While he's giving up revenue at the outset, the mayor agreed to promote his services in the county newsletter and community website, and Tony is seeing an increase in the number of rides overall, not just for the hospital's diabetic patients.

"Furthermore, the assessment identifies patients who are experiencing severe financial difficulties. For this problem, we're negotiating with LaTanya for a discount on Integra's insurance products available to the elderly, as well as those in the "financial hardship" bracket. As you can see, by assessing the social issues that are affecting health, we can provide targeted solutions that are much less costly than reactive care when patients are admitted or readmitted to our hospital.

"The mayor has also agreed to allocate 20 percent of all new business permits to healthy food stores and restaurants in our community. By creating a health-conscious community, Live WELLington will boost home values and real estate taxes and bring other revenue back into the community.

"Sonia Hernandez, Wellington's consumer advocate, is simply delighted with all that is happening now, and she is busy further educating the community—both individuals with diabetes and those potentially at risk—and providing access to community resources. She knows that what we've put in place, and are continuing to work on, is greatly enhancing the health of the community by reducing diabetic disease.

"As for Daria, our patient representative for our ecosystem collaboration team, she has been instrumental in helping to get across the need for all that we're doing and is now personally benefiting from better disease management. Furthermore, as she currently falls into Integra's 'financial hardship' bracket, once it's implemented, Integra will waive the copays and deductibles for treatment if she follows preventative recommendations as part of her diabetic treatment plan.

"Which brings me, finally, to us here at WCH. While we are funding parts of these collaborative solutions—including the physician incentive to conduct the social determinants assessment—we are already seeing higher patient satisfaction and improved community health. These changes warrant our attention. Thus, both the prevalence and rates of diabetes are starting to come down, and our data show that the reduced cost of care will soon be greater than the additional expenses we've incurred.

"While we recognize that keeping people out of our hospital will reduce fee-for-service revenue in the short term, we strongly believe we can shift services to those that promote wellness consistent with value-based payments.

"Let me close with this observation. As this process evolved, I became aware that I was using a completely different set of behaviors to lead the ecosystem collaborative initiative. I was much less directional than I would have been in the past, becoming more of a facilitator as I first sought to align all these vastly different stakeholders around a common purpose. I had to be open to creatively overcoming any barriers and obstacles that stood in the way of achieving the goals we collectively developed. Being aware that this way of leading was indeed different, I was able to apply the new behaviors consistently and consciously.

"These new behaviors are not rocket science, and in many ways, they are common sense. Unfortunately, though, given the way we're wired, common sense is often not that common! However, I found that having a framework that you can use to guide you really helps you to focus and be aware. In time, you too will learn these new skills and will come to think and act differently. Thank you all very much for your time."

After Heather fielded questions and her efforts were applauded by the board and her peers—including Glen—Amy spoke again.

"Anybody can see the immense value in the work Heather has been pursuing. As a result, we now need to think about a completely different operating model for our six hospitals. We need to be sure that everyone sees themselves as a community provider of health and care and wellness, and this perspective drives us to think more broadly about our mission, vision, and values, reconsidering what our role is in the communities we serve. Heather's had her turn, and now we pass the torch to allow you to lead ecosystem collaborations in your community hospitals.

"This will be news to Heather as well, and it's most certainly radical, but with our chief financial officer's full support and blessing, your balanced scorecards will be moving away from a focus on the number of beds filled and revenue per case to reflect new measures that include how much of your total cost of care for your high-cost illnesses you have removed through collaborative relationships. Your performance will also be assessed on the impact and effectiveness of the community health programs you initiate and on what value you create through the partnerships you establish outside of the four walls of your hospital.

"To build on what Heather said about being a convener, I want our hospitals to be a convener of community resources in all our geographic areas with the goal of continuously improving the lives of all the people we are here to serve. For ourselves, I want the H in CHS to not to stand for hospital, but for *health*. And I don't mean just internally. I would like you, our board members, to approve a formal rebranding from Channel Hospital System to Channel Health System."

DECEMBER 2: THE DAY AFTER THE CHS BOARD AND EXECUTIVE LEADERSHIP RETREAT

As she sat back down at her desk, Heather breathed a sigh of relief and allowed herself a smile. It had gone over well, and Amy was very pleased. She put her files and notebook in a drawer in her desk and turned on her monitor. With a shrug, she ignored the new sea of unread emails, and turned to the file she'd been working on before she went to the boardroom. She scanned the list of next steps and nodded as she reread each point:

- Largest community employers: coordinate on-site internist visits for diabetes screening
- Nurse care coordinators: community outreach to learn the best ways to encourage changes in behavior
- Nutritionists: perform home visits (check the fridge and stock with healthy items using vouchers)
- Sonia: community-wide communication of benefits
- LaTanya: pursue National Committee for Quality Assurance accreditation for Integra and boost Healthcare Effectiveness Data and Information Set scores
- Sojin: ask doctors to reach out to schedule visits, form internist/endocrinologist partnerships; continue her work with the patient-centered medical home concept
- Dan: explore bringing a telehealth platform to WCH

Satisfied, she straightened her keyboard and began to type:

Most of our payments are still fee-for-service—talk to Dan and Bijan about harvesting some of the fee-for-service income to fund these programs now to ready us for value-based payments. Reduce recurring costs and develop outpatient programs.

Move slowly. We will continue to go after diabetic care but we need partners to help keep solving the issues. Success now won't eliminate future difficulties.

Keep leading from the HELM!

REFERENCE

McGinnis, J. M., P. Williams-Russo, and J. R. Knickman. 2002. "The Case for More Active Policy Attention to Health Promotion." *Health Affairs* 21 (2): 78–93.

CHAPTER 11

Developing Health Ecosystem Leaders

*If you are under the impression you have already
perfected yourself, you will never rise to the
heights you are no doubt capable of.*

—Kazuo Ishiguro, 1989

IN THE CASE of Wellington Community Hospital, Heather Mitchell was able to work across her ecosystem to build a collaborative solution to a real issue her community was facing, in which her hospital played a significant role. As Heather initially approached her task, she quickly recognized that she would need to engage a different set of skills and behaviors to be successful. She demonstrated great self-awareness and explored new ideas and input from a variety of new resources, including forward-thinking leaders, mentors from inside and outside her organization, and an executive coach. In particular, she did the following:

- Accepted that what made her successful in the past as a hospital president was not sufficient to meet her current and future professional goals or the needs of her hospital and health system.
- Embraced the fact that changing her leadership style required real focus and energy, especially learning and

using new behaviors that were unfamiliar to her and outside her comfort zone.

- Managed her enthusiasm and drive to get to solutions so others had time to express their views and to contribute to and feel ownership of the path forward.
- Modified her role to that of convener and orchestrator of the collaborative effort.
- Knew that acquiring and demonstrating new skills meant that she would not always be successful, at least initially, and that was OK.

The learning Heather received from her readings, the advice from Frank Brady, the coaching from Samantha Geary, and the insights she developed along the way helped her to build her strength as an ecosystem leader. While much of the advice and coaching Heather received seemed relatively straightforward and logical, she was aware that it was not going to be easy to modify long-term habits and perspectives. She was focused and intentional as she began to modify her leadership style from what had worked for her in the past to a new ecosystem leadership context.

Heather's efforts at modifying and developing her leadership style were supported by her emotional intelligence and her learning agility. The attributes of someone who demonstrates emotional intelligence were defined by Daniel Goleman (1998):

- Self-awareness: Can read her own emotions and know her strengths and weaknesses.
- Self-regulation: Able to manage her emotions and motivations effectively. Can adapt to changing situations or emerging obstacles.
- Social awareness: Facile at reading social situations and sensing others' emotions.
- Relationship orientation: Effective at developing and managing relationships with a broad range of people.

Of equal importance, Heather was willing to leave her comfort zone. She enjoyed new situations and challenges, using her interactions with others and her successes and failures to develop new skills. This learning agility—a focus on developing new skills and emotional intelligence—is an important attribute for anyone seeking to grow his health ecosystem leadership model (HELM) capabilities. As Matthew Guy from ReThink Health states, "You need leaders who treat learning as part of their daily activities, who don't just treat the work as something that gets put on the shelf, never to be looked at again. Learning leaders take the time to consider what worked, what didn't work, and how they can take what they've learned from the experience and try something different. Developing leaders with this capacity should be on the forefront of our attention, but it's not something that's going to change overnight. It takes time."

MAKING A START

As we've discussed, ecosystem leadership requires a somewhat different set of skills—and mind-set—than does the approach of a solo sector leader. The good news is that with planning and effort, like what we saw from Heather, the capabilities, behaviors, skills, and knowledge that are required for partnerships and collaborations can be developed and mastered.

Our experience, along with the research of Morgan W. McCall, Michael M. Lombardo, and Ann M. Morrison (1988), suggests that the building of different and new capabilities occurs through a combination of learning situations. We know that new capabilities are best developed through on-the-job experiences. In fact, their research suggests adults ought to spend 70 percent of their development time on such activities (Training Industry 2014). As we saw, Heather was learning and adapting in real time as she pursued her objective.

The time Heather spent with Samantha Geary and Frank Brady illustrates another aspect of this same theory: that 20 percent of development ought to come from learning from other people through coaching, feedback, role models, mentors, and so on. Most of the coaching Heather received occurred in response to events that unfolded as she developed her solution.

As it was in Heather's case, feedback in the context of relevant experience can be significant in the development of new skills. The reading and research Heather did before she went to the conference and what she learned at the conference represents the final 10 percent of development time, which comes from targeted self-improvement through courses and other informative learning resources.

As leadership coaches and talent development practitioners, we have found that behavioral change and the learning of new leadership skills are most successful when a dedicated and time-based plan, with specific action steps, milestones, and targets to be achieved along the way, is in place. Just as we saw with Heather, developing new skills and adapting current skills to new situations requires focus.

We will learn more about that plan at the end of the chapter. For now, we stress that development is not just about managing gaps and improving what we might term *gap areas*. Instead, as we've learned over time, effort should be spent on enhancing our strengths. Effective learning and development plans address how to capitalize on strengths to improve performance in existing and new environments.

What follows in this chapter are suggestions for your own development—and that of your peers and subordinates—for each of the competencies included in our model. The key is to use these suggestions to trigger your thinking and find opportunities to grow and develop that are meaningful to you and your organization. Remember, real development occurs when something that matters is at stake!

LEADERSHIP CAPABILITIES IN THE HEALTH ECOSYSTEM

As you have seen in the earlier chapters, successful leaders in the health ecosystem span the boundaries between organizations and manage the inevitable tensions that characterize relationships between stakeholders with disparate values, perspectives, priorities, and incentives. These leaders envision a future in which a diverse set of stakeholders work together to enhance the health of communities.

They use this vision to identify, reach out to, and bring together the potential stakeholders, and effective ecosystem leaders help these interested parties adapt and align around the shared vision. These leaders facilitate the definition of solutions that use the unique capabilities of each participant to execute that vision.

Creating mutual visions and defining solutions are likely to generate questions and areas of disagreement, conflict, and ambiguity. Ecosystem leaders possess the abilities to confront, discuss, and resolve these issues to move toward a solution. They allow all the stakeholders to be part of designing the actions that will permit them to move forward despite uncertainty, to monitor and learn from the results of their actions, and to use this learning to further develop their approach.

As reflected earlier, HELM comprises four core leadership competencies, and leaders with these ecosystem capabilities can successfully operate in an environment of high interpersonal trust and mutual respect. They espouse innovative thinking and continuous learning, demonstrating the improvement necessary to sustain critical relationships across multiple dimensions and various stakeholders. Working together, these leaders create the new and innovative approaches needed to improve the affordability, quality, and outcomes the various sectors of the health industry seek, and, in turn, they enhance the health of our communities.

USING THIS CHAPTER

As demonstrated by our research and highlighted in the interview quotes throughout the prior chapters, a HELM mind-set and competencies can be learned, developed, and strengthened. This chapter provides you with ideas, resources, and coaching tips specific to each of the four competencies and embedded behaviors of our model to enable you to become a successful ecosystem leader.

The coaching tips identify specific activities you can practice to master each new leadership competency. These are organized around the core attributes for each cluster of the model, as set out in chapters 6 to 9. In our case study, Heather used many of these tips, and we highlight those with asterisks to help illustrate the competency development tip in action. Looking back at the passages in the case study where you saw the behavior will help you visualize it in action, and we also provide some guidance at the end of the section for each competency.

These more specific coaching ideas are followed by some broader development activities that you can use to build your abilities over time. These approaches can also be used by organizations to create a systematic development strategy to build leaders with these abilities. Finally, we offer some suggestions for additional resources, with ideas for further reading to enhance your development in each core cluster.

PART 1: ENVISION THE FUTURE

Generate *What-if* Ideas

1. Resist thinking you know what causes a problem and take the time to understand multiple causes and factors that could contribute to the issue.*
2. Find people who are different from you—in specialty, level, background, viewpoints—and seek their thoughts on the problems you face.*
3. Look for parallel problems in other organizations, particularly those in other sectors in health and beyond, and seek to understand how they see the problem and

what they are trying to accomplish. Identify solutions that have been successful.*

4. Examine how competitors see or do things differently.
5. Take the time to understand how the community (citizens, customers, stakeholders) thinks about the issue.*
6. Ask others to identify and describe what they think is working or not working today.*
7. Create a picture of the ideal end state. Who would be contributing to the solution? What would they be doing? How would people react? What will the customer experience look like? What would be the outcome)?*

Integrate Ideas to Create Innovative Solutions

1. Listen to and acknowledge concerns and weave ideas into the solution.*
2. Look for anomalies when standard solutions do not produce the expected outcome. What do the anomalies have in common? Identify additional factors and stakeholders that should be considered.
3. Question assumptions that people are making and examine your own assumptions. Ask reflective questions.*
4. Debate yourself. What are the issues, arguments, and data that make your ideas work? What are the ones that argue against your ideas?

Advance the Vision

1. Advance and modify your assumptions and ideas as you receive input and learn about different points of view.*
2. Use learning from initial actions to advance and modify your vision.*

3. Feel confident in what you are trying to achieve and be prepared to modify what can be accomplished—multiple times.*

Case Study Learning

1. Note how Heather never jumped into the problem, even when she determined that diabetes was her key issue.
2. Rather than trying to deal with things in the hospital or only in the health sector, she reached out to other people across her community to make sure she was seeing the full picture.
3. She sought to generate empathy with others—she was not alone in having problems, nor were her colleagues. That commonality helped determine where there were mutual issues to be addressed.
4. Heather recognized that as work progressed, the future vision would continue to advance.

Overall Development Activities

To support the development of these behaviors, we offer the following broader and practical development activities:

1. Identify leaders, both from within the health industry and from related sectors, who have a history of ecosystem success. Seek opportunities to spend time with them, discussing their businesses and experiences.
2. Beyond your own sphere, increase your knowledge of the other health industry sectors and of those organizations that affect community health (e.g., public health; policy makers; social agencies, including housing; city planning; education) by reading, making visits, and attending meetings.
3. Volunteer or join the board of a different health sector company, social agency, or not-for-profit organization.

4. Develop your perspective by learning about and understanding ecosystem collaborations outside the industry and participate in outside groups or meetings that bring together people from outside the industry.

5. Seek out learning opportunities related to designing what-if thinking and scenario planning.

6. Take on a tough project that requires a new vision or approach and that others may have tackled without success—be bold and brave!

7. Work on a project that requires exploration of issues that you have not worked on before, ideally identifying projects related to enhancing population health (e.g., housing, food, neighborhood safety, education).

8. Seek opportunities to be a change champion. Look for something that needs to be changed and that you feel is important. Bring the issue forward and enlist others in your efforts.

PART 2: ALIGN STAKEHOLDERS

Seek Connections to Further a Broad Purpose

1. Enlist others in defining the problem and all its elements before generating potential solutions.*

2. Take the time to identify and reach out to the groups and sectors that are interested in a problem you are trying to solve.*

3. Remember that the purpose you start with may not be where you end up.*

4. Share your initial vision in a meaningful and bold way and then seek input—be clear that you expect the vision to evolve as each stakeholder contributes her ideas.*

5. Share your vision with others in a way that considers how they will hear and react to it—make sure you are not too far ahead of people.*

6. When sharing your point of view, be sure to consider what it means for the other stakeholders and their businesses and emphasize opportunities to contribute to shaping the vision.

7. People differ in terms of how they prefer to receive information—headlines versus detail, leading with the bottom line versus building up to your conclusion—and it's important to understand these preferences.

8. Pause to ask how you're doing in terms of pace, amount of information, and so on in early conversations with people you don't know well, and then adjust accordingly.

9. Be open, because openness helps others understand your approach to work, problems, or opportunities—people will get to know you better and be comfortable sharing with you and the group.

10. Practice the art of storytelling—for some, this practice comes naturally, and for others, it is a learned skill, but the beauty is that the stories don't have to be original; you should always have something planned to draw on.

11. Use narrative storytelling to illustrate the shared, urgent challenge and put forth a call to action.

Enable Groups to Come Together to Build Relationships

1. Build in time for people to get to know each other—familiarity helps build trust and makes it more likely that stakeholders will give each other the benefit of the doubt when tensions arise.*

2. Hold initial meetings with stakeholders in person, if possible, and not always in a work setting.*
3. Take the time to learn at least three non-work-related things about each stakeholder and share some of the same things about yourself to establish rapport.
4. Be open, and ask the group to be open, about competing time commitments, and explore ways the group can minimize time conflicts.
5. Practice active listening by giving the speaker your full attention. Literally force yourself to become psychologically silent, and avoid the tendency to reload (mentally preparing your response instead of fully listening).*
6. Sometimes the best way to help people understand is to ask questions—so ask for their viewpoints and what else they think should be considered.*

Demonstrate Respect for a Diversity of Expertise, Perspectives, Interests, and Values

1. Put your assumptions about each organization or sector to the side.
2. Even if you might know the answer already, ask a lot of questions and spend time listening to answers to help generate a belief that people have value to add.
3. Give each stakeholder an opportunity to share her background, priorities, and the skills that she brings to the table.*
4. Take the time to understand the guiding purpose and mission of each stakeholder organization and how it operates to fulfill that mission.*
5. Ask people to describe what their organizations are doing to resolve the specific issue that has been identified, as well as other efforts to improve the health of a population.*

Encourage Open Dialogue and Exchange of Interests, Ideas, Expertise, and Information Among Stakeholders

1. Get everyone involved, paying close attention to the quiet or those reluctant to speak up.*
2. Be confident but don't overstate your position.
3. Share the assumptions you made, what things you ruled out and why.
4. Think out loud and solicit others' input: "Here's what I am thinking. . . . What do you think?"*
5. Test your assumptions by putting them on the table and asking for feedback.*
6. Once you state your opinions, stop and ask others for theirs.*
7. Watch your airtime; be mindful of how much you speak compared to others.
8. Ask more than you tell, and use open questions that solicit a detailed response—avoid closed questions where the answer is only yes or no. Open questions can bring out emotions, opinions, and feelings, whereas closed questions are generally fact-finding.*
9. Don't start by asking what's wrong; focus on what you want to accomplish.
10. Learn what others believe and why they believe it, seeking to understand their goals, motivations, and requirements.*
11. Put yourself in the shoes of others; seek to understand how they formed their viewpoints and what might make it difficult for them to see the situation as you do.*
12. Ask questions to help you understand the views of other stakeholders. What are the important things going on in their organizations? How do their organizations operate? What do they measure and reward?

13. Don't draw conclusions too quickly or dismiss others' ideas, but ask more questions and pause to see what others say.

14. Allow others to talk without interruption.

15. Demonstrate understanding by restating the opinions of others as clearly as they expressed their ideas.

16. Look for views from others that you can agree with and reinforce those beliefs.

Case Study Learning

1. Heather ensured she defined the problem based on numerous inputs before any solutions were considered.

2. She took the time to identify the interested parties and shared her vision so that others could contribute to it.

3. Time was always given for her stakeholders to get to know one another, and she sought to hold her meetings in social settings as well as business settings.

4. She actively sought to make sure that she was listening and asked questions as she encouraged others to do so, ensuring everyone had the chance to speak and contribute.

5. Everyone involved was encouraged by Heather to discuss the problem from his perspective and to share his efforts to address diabetes thus far.

6. When Sonia was quiet, Heather encouraged her to speak up. Heather found ways for Phillipe to help, rather than hinder, by testing her own and his assumptions using open questions.

7. Heather made sure that everyone understood each other's goals as she shared her own to ensure clarity.

Overall Development Activities

1. Seek opportunities to influence during situations in which you have no authority.

2. Lead diverse teams in solving difficult problems.

3. Work with or lead a team to integrate diverse systems, processes, or procedures.

4. Manage a temporary team involved in a turnaround where a new solution is required.

5. Seek opportunities to work and lead work across the organization (e.g., across functions, in multiple geographies, across product lines).

6. Learn about the business models of the other key health sector players and about their customers—how their customers' needs are being met, the products and services the organizations offer, how revenue is generated, their cost structures, their organizational structures, their key metrics, their sources of profitability, and so on.

PART 3: MANAGE BOUNDARIES AND OBSTACLES

Support Constructive Conflict

1. If they remain unspoken, publicly discuss difficult issues that could put the effort in jeopardy, and be prepared to deal with how people react.

2. Don't be defensive even if you feel attacked; seek to calm the situation instead by asking clarifying questions about what you can do to help move things forward.

3. Think about the long-term goal and purpose, and don't be distracted by immediate concerns.

4. Speak to others the way you would want to be spoken to; avoid critical statements.

5. Present the problem so the likelihood of others productively engaging is consistent with why you think the issue is important.*

6. Present your reasons and concerns before presenting your solutions.*

7. List the areas of disagreement and then take the time to understand why those areas are important to the different parties.

8. If discussions lead to an impasse, step back and ask yourself and the group to consider the consequences of not overcoming it by agreeing on a mutually beneficial solution.

Focus on Opportunities in the Face of Disagreements and Setbacks

1. Do not postpone the difficult discussions, because this delay gives space for more misunderstanding and miscommunication to occur between the parties, making challenges harder to resolve.*

2. List all the areas of agreement before focusing on disagreements.

3. Focus on issues you have in common and seek solutions that are equitable for multiple stakeholders.

4. Seek out the unique value that needs to be delivered, not the activities. Notice this distinction: "creating a superb experience for families of residents" rather than "conducting new resident family orientation sessions."

5. Have confidence in your professional gut, and don't be afraid to disagree respectfully with someone who carries a higher title.

6. Stick to your guns in the face of pushback when data and experience tell you you're right. You will be respected for holding your own.

7. View conflict as an opportunity and remember that healthy debate usually leads to a better outcome (while consensus can often lead to a diluted decision).

8. Learn to disagree without being disagreeable! Use open questions to fully elicit the other person's views before

sharing your own—this technique sets you up to identify common ground and share where you agree before stating your disagreement.

9. Determine what is vitally important to other stakeholders—what are their must-haves?*

10. Look for ways to minimize the negative impact of specific solutions on each stakeholder.

Resolve Points of Tension, Critical Interfaces, and Role Confusion

1. Maintain your composure in the face of pushback, reminding yourself that the goal is to attack problems, not people.

2. In the face of unresolved conflict, seek out a third way that is slightly different from either party's initial positions.

3. Expect problems and tension—stay focused on what you want to achieve and be prepared to resolve the conflict.*

4. Seek opportunities to give confidence to the other stakeholders that will satisfy the overall interests of the group.*

5. Think about the major objections that stakeholders are likely to raise and be prepared to respond.

6. Mentally rehearse for tough situations, learn to recognize those that might trigger your disruptive behaviors, and be prepared to react more effectively.*

7. Base what you say on facts, not emotions or opinion—if you don't have enough facts you may want to wait until you do.

8. Be flexible and explore alternatives, as this adaptability will provide more space for adjustments. Knowing the pros and cons of alternative solutions will help the group make the most suitable decision.

9. Be sure that all stakeholders are clear on the benefits they will realize from the solution.

10. Respond to objections and the disruptive behavior of others in ways that maintain focus on what you are trying to achieve and keep the effort on track.*

Case Study Learning

1. When seeking to get Dan on board, Heather presented her situation from his perspective as she shared her problems.

2. When Phillipe was acting in a way that was detrimental to the overall goals of the group, she immediately tackled the problem and developed solutions that benefited everyone.

3. Whenever something occurred that could potentially derail her efforts, Heather found ways to maintain focus.

4. When presenting to her peers, she ensured that the benefits being presented far outweighed any objections anyone may have.

Overall Development Activities

1. Actively look for opportunities to become involved in tough negotiations.

2. Lead the charge on a controversial issue.

3. Position yourself as a change agent; build the business case for a change or a cause you believe in and commit to bringing necessary stakeholders on board.

PART 4: ACT AND LEARN

Plan Action Steps Jointly with Diverse Stakeholders

1. Be open to modifying or giving up some of your interests or solutions to achieve the common goal.*

2. Clearly define the problem you want to solve and present the value of your solution so others understand how it will help achieve the goal.
3. Engage all key stakeholders in building the plan.
4. Ensure that all parties involved understand what is intended to be accomplished and any associated risks. Risk is more palatable when people can say, "We're all in this together."
5. Recognize that smaller actions are ways to learn, manage risks, and move toward the ultimate vision.

Enact Concrete Steps to Advance the Vision

1. Break the issue into all its components and look for ways to create order.*
2. Make the process transparent to all participants so there is a shared understanding of what will be done and of the objectives and measures.
3. Define what needs to be done and set final and progress goals and measures.
4. Expand your learning opportunities by attempting multiple smaller experiments.*
5. Test your theories and ideas as simply and inexpensively as you can, particularly in the early stages.
6. Build and articulate the business case for the risks you take and be driven by the potential gain when the risk pays off.
7. Don't try to get it totally right the first time. The more complex and uncertain the situation, the more you need to be incremental; make smaller decisions and seek quicker feedback.*

Act Despite Uncertainty

1. Remember there are inherent risks that can result from doing nothing—it's better to try and fail than to avoid any action.*
2. Recognize that every risk won't pay off—create an environment in your team where it is OK to fail and learn from mistakes.
3. Expect the unexpected.

Use Feedback from Actions Taken to Adapt, Plan Next Steps, and Advance the Vision

1. Set expectations early on that adapting the approach and vision is an expected part of the process.
2. Define minor checkpoints, share promising results as well as failures, measure progress in small steps, and celebrate wins.*
3. Use postaction reviews to generate learning. What were your objectives? Why did you not achieve those objectives? What part of the solution worked? What should be different the next time?
4. Seek common elements in successes and failures and integrate those elements into next steps.
5. Before eliminating or changing a solution that did not produce the desired results, identify any positive attributes that you want to retain.
6. When seeking feedback ask, Are there changes that make sense? Do we need to define the issue differently? Should we eliminate or recombine some of our solution elements?

7. Revisit your initial problem statement and solutions, and question whether you should redefine the problem and look for some new solutions.

8. As plans change, remain focused on achieving the ultimate goals and help the group stay focused.*

9. When an approach does not work, demonstrate your continued commitment to the overall purpose and goals— look at what can be learned and use that information to change the plan or approach.*

10. Use learning to advance the vision, identify new stakeholders, and modify the approach.*

Case Study Learning

1. Heather remained flexible when it came to developing solutions and sought to find different, smaller components that contributed to solutions for the overall problem.

2. She was not afraid to try things out and see what occurred; she expected that things might change.

3. She understood that small steps were all part of generating much broader successes, and that they are a way to maintain momentum.

4. Regular meetings were planned so that all her stakeholders could see the progress being made, and thus she maintained their enthusiasm.

5. Heather's commitment never wavered, and her response to potential setbacks was always to see them as an opportunity for forward motion, keeping the overall vision and end goals in mind.

Overall Development Activities

1. Become involved in or lead continuous improvement initiatives.

2. Volunteer to lead or participate in a new initiative.

3. Relaunch an existing service or initiative that is not doing well.

4. Study innovations. Do you see any patterns in successful innovations? How about in innovation failures?

ENSURING THE BEST DEVELOPMENT STRATEGY

As alluded to at the beginning of the chapter, we all have strengths and areas in which we can improve. We recommend that, at any one time, your development action plan focus on no more than four areas: one or two high-priority and current strengths to leverage, and one or two emerging aspects that require focused attention. We further recommend developing HELM skills through the lens of the 70-20-10 approach discussed earlier in the chapter.

You can use the coaching tips in this chapter as a starting point to identify which HELM capabilities you want to target for development.

- Review the behaviors in each of the competency clusters (see exhibit 5.1). How would you rate yourself? Which behaviors are strengths that you consistently demonstrate? Which abilities do you demonstrate, at least in certain situations, and now need to use more frequently or in more situations? Which are behaviors that you need to develop and practice?
- Ask others who see you in your leadership capacity (your managers, peers, direct reports, customers, other key stakeholders) to provide you with feedback on these behaviors.
- Seek an opportunity to participate in a leadership assessment focused on Goleman's five-factor personality model (Goleman 1998) to assess emotional intelligence. Employ other personality inventories, such as the Hogan Leadership Forecast Series or the EQi 2.0.
- Use the feedback you receive to identify strengths to leverage and areas that need to be developed. Create strategies to minimize gaps.

- Create your plan. The template in exhibit 11.1 provides a good framework. The coaching, development ideas, and resources from this chapter can be used to define the specific actions and steps you can take to achieve your goals. Remember, the best plans have a strong focus on experiences, and they factor in support from mentors; coaches; and additional resources such as books, webinars, TED talks, and conferences.

As you determine your options for real developmental progress, we suggest you consider the following questions:

- Would leveraging these strengths significantly affect ecosystem solutions for your organization?
- For each development area, what short- or long-term benefits do you see from improvements?
- How can you leverage your strengths to raise the bar on your performance and have a positive impact, and what is the potential reward for your effort?

Exhibit 11.1: Sample Development Plan

INDIVIDUAL DEVELOPMENT ACTION PLAN			
Name: Date:			
Development Opportunities	Available Resources or Support	Success Defined	Target Date(s)

- Is this something you don't know how to do, or is this something you can already demonstrate and need to practice more and improve?
- Is this something that you do reasonably well but is invisible to other people, or that you don't use as frequently as you could?
- Is there something you're not doing because there are obstacles and disincentives or because it's a low priority for you?

Having answered these questions and designed your initial plan, you need to ensure that it is realistic and therefore achievable. To assess the plan's practicality, we recommend you consider another set of questions:

- If you need to learn or practice something, how do you prefer to learn things—for example, through hands-on experience, courses, books, a mentor?
- If the issue is not skill development, what needs to happen to turn this development area into a strength? The solution might be about removing obstacles or changing your priorities.
- Is your action plan realistic, given other job demands and constraints?
- What is your timing to develop this competency?
- Is this development area a priority? Will lack of this competency limit your career choices?
- What results do you expect as you accomplish your development plan?
- How will you hold yourself accountable? Do you have access to an accountability partner or coach?
- How will you measure your success?

MEASURE YOUR PROGRESS AND CONTINUOUSLY IMPROVE

As the last bullet point in the list suggests, whatever makes it into your plan must be measurable to enable you to assess your progress. You can use simple measurement criteria such as the frequency with which you tried a new behavior, from never to daily, when you need some way to track your development to stay focused and motivated. For tracking, use the familiar but relevant tool of formulating SMART goals (specific, measurable, attainable, relevant, time bound).

We recognize that behavioral change is hard to measure for yourself, and that's why we recommend you actively seek the feedback of others. For example, if you are working with a coach or a mentor, she can observe you and provide feedback. You may also let others in the ecosystem solution group know what behaviors you want to demonstrate and why you think those behaviors are important, and seek their feedback.

This approach has the added benefit of modeling what good ecosystem leadership looks like and shows an openness that can build trust and relationships with others in the group. Again, the most important thing is to measure your progress and ask your key stakeholders to provide suggestions for future development as well—don't rely totally on self-observance to determine what needs fixing. We suggest looking into the Feed*Forward* Tool, as developed by leadership guru Marshall Goldsmith (2018).

WHY BOTHER?

Developing your abilities as a HELM leader in the health ecosystem is critical to improving value, affordability, and the lives of people in the communities you serve. The ideas in this chapter will support you in your efforts to create the robust, high-value ecosystem solutions needed to enhance population health. As we heard from David Carmouche of Ochsner: "We need many more people with the ability to foster cross-sector collaboration. This is a skill set that can be developed. The reason these leadership skills are so important is because once you create an understanding and accurate perceptions, a lot of the resistance barriers dissipate quickly. I would say that we would all make progress if we had more people who had the skills and capabilities to reach across sectors and put themselves in the other side's shoes."

REFERENCES

Goldsmith, M. 2018. "FeedForward." Accessed June 4. www.marshall goldsmithfeedforward.com/html/FeedForward-Tool.htm.

Goleman, D. 1998. *Working with Emotional Intelligence.* New York: Bantam Books.

McCall, M. W., M. M. Lombardo, and A. M. Morisson. 1988. *The Lessons of Experience: How Successful Executives Develop on the Job.* Lanham, MD: Lexington Books.

Training Industry. 2014. "The 70:20:10 Model for Learning and Development." Published January 28. https://training industry.com/wiki/content-development/the-702010-model -for-learning-and-development/.

SUGGESTED READINGS

Envision the Future

Anthony, S. D. 2012. *The Little Black Book of Innovation: How It Works, How to Do It.* Boston: Harvard Business Review Press.

Chamorro-Premuzic, T. 2015. "You Can Teach Someone to Be More Creative." *Harvard Business Review.* Published February 23. https:// hbr.org/2015/02/you-can-teach-someone-to-be-more-creative.

Christensen, C. M. 2013. *The Innovator's Dilemma: When New Technologies Cause Great Firms to Fail.* Boston: Harvard Business Review Press.

Christensen, C. M., and M. E. Raynor. 2013. *The Innovator's Solution: Creating and Sustaining Successful Growth.* Boston: Harvard Business Review Press.

Cornell University. 2018. *Leading Through Creativity* [online course]. Accessed June 8. https://sha.cornell.edu/app/execed/system /pdfs/10088/original/DLP04LSM507_Leading_through_ Creativity.pdf.

Edmondson, A. C., and S. Salter Reynolds. 2016. *Building the Future: Big Teaming for Audacious Innovation.* Oakland, CA: Berrett-Koehler.

Gryskiewicz, S., and S. Taylor. 2007. *Making Creativity Practical: Innovation That Gets Results.* New York: Wiley.

Mauborgne, R., and Kim, W. C. 2004. "Blue Ocean Strategy." *Harvard Business Review.* Published October 1. https://hbr.org /product/blue-ocean-strategy/an/R0410D-PDF-ENG.

Sloane, P. 2007. *The Innovative Leader: How to Inspire Your Team and Drive Creativity.* Philadelphia: Kogan Page.

Von Oech, R. 1998. *A Whack on the Side of the Head: How You Can Be More Creative.* New York: Warner Books.

Whitney, D. K., and A. Trosten-Bloom. 2010. *The Power of Appreciative Inquiry: A Practical Guide to Positive Change*, 2nd ed. San Francisco: Berrett-Koehler.

Align Stakeholders

Abrashoff, D. M. 2012. *It's Your Ship: Management Techniques from the Best Damn Ship in the Navy*, rev. ed. New York: Business Plus.

Cartwright, T., and D. Baldwin. 2006. *Communicating Your Vision.* Greensboro, NC: Center for Creative Leadership.

Covey, S. M. R. 2008. *The Speed of Trust: The One Thing That Changes Everything.* New York: Free Press.

Edmondson, A. C., and S. Salter Reynolds. 2016. *Building the Future: Big Teaming for Audacious Innovation.* Oakland, CA: Berrett-Koehler.

Ernst, C., and D. Chrobot-Mason. 2011. *Boundary Spanning Leadership: Six Practices for Solving Problems, Driving Innovation, and Transforming Organizations.* New York: McGraw-Hill.

Gallo, C. 2011. "The 7 Secrets of Inspiring Leaders." *Forbes.* Published July 6. www.forbes.com/sites/carminegallo/2011/07/06/the-7-secrets-of-inspiring-leaders/#63966e031433.

Halpern, B. L., and K. Lubar. 2003. *Leadership Presence: Dramatic Techniques to Reach Out, Motivate, Inspire.* New York: Gotham Books.

Lasley, M. 2004. *Courageous Visions: How to Unleash Passionate Energy in Your Life and Your Organization.* Anaheim, CA: Discover Press.

Rethink Health. 2015a. *Public Narrative: Story of Now Individual Tool.* Published November 5. www.rethinkhealth.org/wp-content/uploads/2015/11/story-of-now-individual-practice-11-05.pdf.

Rethink Health. 2015b. *Public Narrative: Story of Self.* Published November 5. www.rethinkhealth.org/wp-content/uploads/2015/11/Story-of-Self-11-5.pdf.

Richardson, A. 2011. "Collaboration Is a Team Sport, and You Need to Warm Up." *Harvard Business Review.* Published May 31. https://hbr.org/2011/05/collaboration-is-a-team-sport.

Sawyer, R. K. 2007. *Group Genius: The Creative Power of Collaboration.* New York: Basic Books.

Manage Boundaries and Obstacles

Marcus, L. J., B. C. Dorn, and E. J. McNulty. 2011. *Renegotiating Health Care: Resolving Conflict to Build Collaboration*, 2nd ed. San Francisco: Jossey-Bass.

Patterson, K., J. Grenny, R. McMillan, and A. Switzer. 2002. *Crucial Conversations: Tools for Talking When Stakes Are High*. New York: McGraw Hill.

Act and Learn

Anthony, S. D. 2009. *The Silver Lining: An Innovation Playbook for Uncertain Times*. Boston: Harvard Business Review Press.

Edmondson, A. C., and S. Salter Reynolds. 2016. *Building the Future: Big Teaming for Audacious Innovation*. Oakland, CA: Berrett-Koehler.

Gill, L. 2009. *You Unstuck: Mastering the New Rules of Risk-Taking in Work and Life*. Palo Alto, CA: Solas House.

Heath, R. 2009. *Celebrating Failure: The Power of Taking Risks, Making Mistakes, and Thinking Big*. Franklin Lakes, NJ: Career Press.

Hodgson, P., and R. P. White. 2001. *Relax, It's Only Uncertainty: Lead the Way When the Way Is Changing*. Indianapolis: FT Press.

Johnson, L. K. 2008. "Increase the Odds of Being Right." *Harvard Business Review*. Published February 28. https://hbr.org/2008/02/increase-the-odds-of-being-rig-1.

Pallotta, D. 2011. "Taking a Risk Is Not Immoral." *Harvard Business Review*. Published August 4. https://hbr.org/2011/08/taking-a-risk-is-not-immoral.

Pillay, S. 2014. "A Better Way to Think About Risk." *Harvard Business Review*. Published December 23. https://hbr.org/2014/12/a-better-way-to-think-about-risk.

Slywotzky, A. 2008. "What Are the Risks You Should Be Taking?" *Harvard Business Review*. February 27. https://hbr.org/2008/02/what-are-the-risks-you-should-1.

Sundheim, D. 2013. *Taking Smart Risks: How Sharp Leaders Win When Stakes Are High*. New York: McGraw-Hill.

Final Word

THERE'S NOT A day that goes by without another big news flash about the state of health in our country. We're inundated with news that is critical of the failures of a broken system that does not provide equity, quality, or affordability. On the other hand, we also hear from innovative thinkers who espouse the opportunities that can be realized with creative problem solving and unique partnerships and collaborations.

People both inside and outside the industry know that the transformation of healthcare is a critical issue for our country. Transformation is both dynamic and extremely complex, and it's unlikely there will be a cure-all solution. There are far too many important and diverse players who need to partner with each other if we are going to make a lasting impact on the health of our nation.

The leaders who do move us to a better future will change how the multiple sectors that affect health work with each other. These health leaders will act, learn, reenvision, realign, and overcome obstacles that will enable them to create solutions that keep people healthy. They will focus on wellness for all while enhancing treatment for those who are sick.

Ecosystem leaders will continuously seek ways to connect, to try new things, and to learn what works and what doesn't in an effort to redefine the industry. Whether they run hospitals, physician groups, insurance companies, pharmaceutical companies, or medical device organizations, these leaders will recognize that the business of caring for people when they are ill or suffering is only part of the business of health. They will step up to the challenge of supporting better health because that is the mission they signed up for. They will move us from the industry of *healthcare* to a focus on both *health* and *care*.

Our main message is that leadership is the key ingredient to ecosystem success. For any real and dramatic changes to the industry to stick, leaders need the mind-set and skill set we have described. That's the bottom line. That's why we wrote this book. We hope it helps to motivate you, your teams, your organizations, and the various sectors that affect the industry to work toward healthier and more productive lives for the people in our country.

We leave you with these few collective observations as you pursue solutions ecosystem. *Every* leader in *our* health industry needs to

- reframe her focus from *healthcare* to *health* and *care*;
- create value for customers through innovative programs and services, regardless of what is regulated;
- build cross-sector collaborative relationships that create sustainable solutions to enhance the health of the nation; and
- take the time and demonstrate the energy and focus needed to develop a health ecosystem leadership mind-set and skill set—it is extraordinarily important, and it is most certainly achievable.

About the Authors

TRACY L. DUBERMAN, PHD, FACHE, PCC

With a background combining her executive experiences in the health industry, two decades of coaching and consulting, and innovative research on executive and physician leadership effectiveness, Tracy founded The Leadership Development (TLD) Group, Inc., and serves as its CEO. TLD Group works with leaders to align talent in order to execute strategy and improve performance through educational workshops; tailored on-site leadership development programs; and personalized, individual coaching for physician and health industry leaders.

Tracy has been recognized as an expert on leadership across the health ecosystem. She speaks on ecosystem leadership, physician leadership, succession planning, and talent development. Before founding TLD Group, Tracy led the organizational effectiveness and healthcare practice at a leading boutique executive coaching firm and was a senior consultant with Hay Group, one of the world's most respected leadership and talent development organizations.

Tracy earned her PhD in public health policy and management from New York University, her MPH from the University of Medicine and Dentistry of New Jersey, and her BA from the University of Rochester. She serves on the board of the Physician Coaching Institute, and she is a Fellow of the American College of Healthcare Executives (FACHE) and of the Harvard McLean Hospital Institute of Coaching. She belongs to the Healthcare Businesswomen's Association and the American College of Physician Executives.

ROBERT SACHS, PHD

Bob works with organizations to enhance and integrate critical leadership talent strategies and systems and to assist them in developing their learning strategies and governance. He also provides coaching to executives. He currently serves as advisory board chair for The Leadership Development (TLD) Group. He also sits on the board of We Care Services for Children. We Care provides mental health and developmental services to children in the San Francisco Bay area. He serves on the advisory board of Pandexio, whose technology supports the development and sharing of critical thinking across organizations.

Bob spent 19 years at Kaiser Permanente (KP), most recently as vice president of national learning and development. His responsibilities at KP included succession management and leadership development. He led the team that provided learning services, including the enterprisewide learning management system, and designed learning solutions for KP's national functions.

Prior to joining KP, Bob was vice president and managing director of the Hay Group. He held national practice leadership and general management roles during his career with Hay. Bob received his BS in psychology from Union College (New York), his MEd in counseling from the University of Hartford, and his PhD in counseling psychology from the University of Pennsylvania.